Egg Decoration

Egg Decoration

by
SUSAN BYRD

DOVER PUBLICATIONS, INC., *New York*

Edited by Aline Becker and Carolyn Detert

Color Photography by:
Sinclair Rogers
Monett, Missouri 65708

Copyright © 1984, 1991 by Susan Byrd.
All rights reserved under Pan American and International Copyright Conventions.

Published in Canada by General Publishing Company, Ltd., 30 Lesmill Road, Don Mills, Toronto, Ontario.

Egg Decoration, first published by Dover Publications, Inc., in 1991, is a republication of *Basic Eggery*, first published by "Eggs by Byrd," Mountain Home, Arkansas in 1984. Minor corrections have been made for this edition.

Manufactured in the United States of America
Dover Publications, Inc., 31 East 2nd Street, Mineola, N.Y. 11501

Library of Congress Cataloging-in-Publication Data

Byrd, Susan.
    Egg decoration / by Susan Byrd.
        p. cm.
    Rev. ed. of: Basic eggery. c1984.
    Includes index.
    ISBN 0-486-26804-7 (pbk.)
    1. Egg decoration.   I. Byrd, Susan. Basic eggery.   II. Title.
TT896.7.B97   1991
745.594'4—dc20
                                                91-13440
                                                 CIP

DEDICATED TO ALL EGGERS EVERYWHERE!

With a special thanks to my parents who provided a quiet place to work, and my husband who encouraged me and put up with my absences!

". . . And the life which I now live in the flesh I live by the faith of the Son of God, who loved me, and gave himself for me."

Galatians 2:20

TABLE OF CONTENTS

Egg Decoration

❧ INTRODUCTION ❧

Welcome to the exciting and challenging world of egg decorating! If you are looking for a new form of expression, a new canvas on which to apply your talents, egg decorating could very well be for you! I sincerely hope that you will find in it the same pleasure and satisfaction that has kept me fascinated since 1966! Hopefully, this book will help you along, making your egg decorating easy and fun right from the start!

Egg decorating is very different from anything you may have tried before, and though it may not be something everyone would like to try, it is something that everyone likes to see! The very fact that relatively few people are doing eggs helps to preserve its uniqueness.

To me, it is so exciting and rewarding, and above all, so very individual, that I suppose I think everyone ought to be as enthralled with it as I am! For instance, if you knit or crochet (which I have done a lot of and have enjoyed!) you are doing the same mechanical thing over and over until you are finished, and then you have an afghan or sweater to go along with all the other afghans and sweaters you have in the closet. Not so with egg decorating! You take a bit of Nature, the egg, and create something beautiful from it, and, whether it is functional or simply decorative, you have created a work of art which will be noticed! Point out an afghan you have just finished and you will get a sincere "How nice". But just point to the clock on the mantle and let it be known that you made it from an ostrich egg, and watch what happens! Instant, wide eyed fascination! And instant conversation when you are stuck for something to talk about! I could go on and on, but by now you must know how I feel about eggery! It is wonderful, and there is no finer group of people than those who do it. We welcome you to join us!

If you are still interested (surely you are!) then keep reading!

This book is designed to teach you the basic techniques a new egger needs to know, starting right at square one.

Included in the book will be a brief history of egg decorating, a description of the eggs available, information on tools and other supplies, and how-to's on everything from emptying an egg to decorating it. There will be projects with instructions and illustrations for completing several different eggs, starting with simpler ones and gradually working up to some that will be more challenging. When you reach the project section, gather up all the supplies called for in each project and work through it from start to finish. Each one is designed to teach you new skills that will enable you to move on to more advanced eggs.

If you have an opportunity to attend a seminar for beginners, by all means, do so! For most people, seminars are one of the best ways to learn because of the hands-on experience, and the fact that there is someone to answer questions and offer advice. In this book, I will attempt to anticipate any questions you may have and to answer them as clearly as possible.

When I teach a seminar, I have three goals in mind for my students. First is to have a good time, second is to learn something new, and third is to go home with an egg they are proud of. I have the same goals in mind for you as you read this book, that you enjoy it, learn from it, and create great eggs because of it!

If you obtained this book from an egg decorating supply house, it is fairly safe to assume that you already know where you can get the eggs and other supplies that will be mentioned later. In the event that you do not know of a place to buy your supplies, please feel free to write to me at the address given on page 36.

CHAPTER I ❧ HISTORY

It is surprising how many people have never heard of egg decorating, or perhaps heard of it, but have never seen it. A typical conversation about eggs might go something like this: A new acquaintance wants to know about your hobbies and you tell them "I do eggs". There will be a little pause while your words soak in, and then they will politely ask, "You do what?" (Your words really didn't soak in at all.) So you answer, just as politely, "I decorate eggshells." Now you can see a glimmer of understanding in their eyes! And you know very well they are thinking "Easter Eggs". Well, just keep cool, and explain to them that what you do with eggs is in no way related to the mental image they have just conjured up of the typical dyed Easter Egg! And you might as well drag out your egg pictures to illustrate your words. Otherwise, they will never understand!

If you really have their attention now, or if they can't get away, just go ahead and give them your whole speech. They will be interested to know that egg decorating isn't new, even though they have never heard of it before. On the contrary, history shows that it began in ancient times, long before the time of Christ. The first recorded mention of it dates back to ancient China, when colored eggs were given during spring fertility festivals. As the mysterious source of new life, the egg was thought to have great magical powers, and thus was held in awe and reverence by many ancient peoples.

Over the centuries the art of egg decorating became more sophisticated. By the thirteenth century gold leafed eggs were known to have been presented to the English Court by King Edward I, and by the sixteenth century eggs with "surprises" in them had come into existence. Eggs were very popular among European nobility of this era, and by the reign of Louis the XV the decorating and giving of eggs was widespread, especially in France.

Practically every country has its version of the decorated egg, and today we can see the special styles and techniques each has developed, and handed down through the ages. One style which must be mentioned is the jeweled style, made famous by Peter Carl Faberge, jeweler to the Russian Court during the late eighteen hundreds and early nineteen hundreds. His Imperial Easter Eggs, made between 1884 and 1916, were not, however, made of actual eggshells, but of precious metals and jewels, fashioned into intricately beautiful, egg-shaped works of art. These eggs have been a joy and an inspiration to the modern day egg artist.

Egg art, as we know it in this country, is fairly young, only really beginning to emerge within the last twenty years or so. There were egg projects, such as Easter egg trees, etc., being done much earlier than this, but few eggs were being done then the way they are today.

There is seemingly no end to the variety of eggs that are being done today, and a good way to see them is to visit one of the many egg shows held around the country each year! (An egg show is an exciting event, even for those who never plan to become an egger!) The huge variety of styles and techniques will have your head buzzing with new ideas of your own!

Usually there are seminars held in conjunction with shows, and, as I mentioned before, seminars are one of the best ways to learn, (notwithstanding great instruction books like this one!) If you have a chance to take a seminar, by all means do so. Choose one that will be a challenge to you, but not be too advanced.

CHAPTER II ✎ POINTS TO CONSIDER

First, keep in mind that eggery is, after all, just a hobby, and perfection isn't the name of the game. But don't get me wrong! I want you to do the very best that you can. In fact I expect it of you! I would like for you to work hard at doing a good job, but not to the point that it becomes a chore and the pleasure is lost. When that happens, it is time to draw the line. The idea is to enjoy what you are doing, and feel relaxed about it!

Point Two; Always remember that no two people do anything just alike. Some are confident and move right ahead, while others may be more timid and require more help. Some will choose one tool to do a job, others will use something else, and so on. All these differences are perfectly OK! After all, this is what makes variety in our lives. (How dull things would be without variety!) So don't worry if you are a little slower than someone else! The very fact that you are slower might just put you in a position to profit by the mistakes and snags the speedier ones could run into! Simply take your time, do the best you can, and enjoy yourself! Also, don't be concerned if your egg isn't as perfect as someone else's. Just remember that you have learned on it, and can always do another one better. People are always their own worst critics. The flaws you can see, simply because you know they are there, would rarely be noticed by someone else, because they are seeing the egg as a whole and not concentrating on one tiny aspect of it.

Next, be aware that some people are inventers, and some aren't. Some will be able to design all their own eggs with ease, while others will be more comfortable working with kits and instructions. If you are one who falls in the first group of people, fantastic! Let your imagination go, because it will be your only limiting factor, and you will thoroughly enjoy doing your own designs. If you are one who falls in the second category, you will derive great pleasure and satisfaction from completing eggs from kits or instructions. Don't for a minute think that there is no challenge in this! For one thing, it nearly always leads to the development of some ideas of your own, either for modifying the egg you are working on, or for creating an entirely new one. In spite of yourself, sooner or later, you will find that you are doing a bit of creating of your own!

One nice thing to keep in mind is that, even though you might be doing an egg designed by someone else, it will still have your own special touch, simply because YOU are the one who made it!

Point Four; Take advantage of artistic talents you may have already developed. For instance, if you have been a painter, you will find that you can paint on eggs. Many of my first eggs had landscapes done in watercolor, because painting in watercolor was "my thing" before getting started in eggery. And I still do a painted egg once in a while, just because I love to paint.

Eggs will accept watercolor, oils, acrylics, stains, metallic waxes, ceramic pastels, pen & ink, and dyes (both natural and man-made). You can quill on them, gold leaf them, decoupage them, bead them, boutique them, antique them, and cover them with everything from fabric to pearl flakes, laces to ribbons, braids to naturals. Just use your imagination! There's no end to it!

Next, Point Five; As you develop in your egging, you will have many ideas for new eggs. Write them down! Do this even if you don't think the idea has merit at the time, because later you may very well find yourself wishing you had saved it. Many of the ideas I develop are "dreamed up" at night after I have gone to bed, so I keep a pad of paper and pen by the bed to scribble notes and sketches on. (My poor husband is used to sleeping with the covers pulled over his eyes!) Also, keep yourself open to new ideas and tips from unexpected sources. You never know when you will have an opportunity to learn something new. For instance, when I first started teaching seminars, I found out very quickly that I would not only be teaching my students, but that I would be learning from them as well. Again, I say, write things down!

Point Six; This point concerns the Murphy's Law that we all know and love so well. You know the one. It says that if anything can go wrong, it will go wrong. Well, believe it, because, as with most endeavors, the course of egg decorating doesn't always run smooth! Anything can happen, and probably will, so be prepared to take it in stride and keep cool. No matter how bad it is, it is never so bad that it can not be helped. (Well, almost never . . .)

To end this, I am including a trouble-shooting section in the book, which I think will help you overcome some of the more common problems you will run across from time to time. Hopefully this will help keep you out of the tranquilizer bottle, and your egg off the ceiling.

Point Seven; Be neat! It is all right to make mistakes as you learn, but do learn by them! The most beautiful egg can be ruined by simple things like smeared glue, carelessly applied trims, etc. There is no need for this to happen. Just remember to take your time, be observant, and immediately correct any mistakes you find. If you are going to take the time to do an egg, take the time to do it right!

Point Eight: These are all the usual bits of advice that have always been given in every instruction book ever written since time out of mind. They must have merit, by virtue of repetition if nothing else, so I am going to repeat them here: use good lighting when you work; be organized (!); if possible, work in a relaxing environment where you can leave your mess indefinately; have the right tools and supplies on hand; and save everything that might some day be useful!

Finally Point Nine: If you have had previous experience doing eggs, you may have learned techniques different from some taught here. If those techniques work for you, and you are happy with them, don't change them. There is more than one way to do nearly anything, and I am only teaching the methods that have worked for me. I am still learning too!

CHAPTER III ❧ THE EGG ITSELF

In starting this section of the book, I am going to pretend that you know next to nothing about eggs, (except that they are usually edible), and work from there.

Chicken eggs may be the most familiar to you, and the easiest to come by, but they are by no means the only choice an egg decorater has! There is an infinate variety of eggs available to us. Some are as small as a bean, some as large as a canteloupe. Some are white, while others may be brown, blue, green or black.

Please allow me to get serious for a moment, (the only time this will happen, I promise!) I have just mentioned the fact that there is a large variety of eggs available, but please note that NONE of the eggs I am going to tell you about should ever be taken from the wild. They are all available from domestic sources, such as game bird farms and hatcheries.

With a few exceptions, ALL wild birds are "protected," which means it is illegal to take their eggs under any circumstances. Two birds which are not protected are the English Sparrow and the Starling. This is because they are not native American birds, and are nuisance birds as well, so it is all right to use their eggs. There may be other birds, in addition to these, which are not protected, but if you are in doubt at all, please do not take the eggs! Let's be good stewards of our beautiful wild birds! Many thanks, both from me and from our wild feathered friends!

Following is a list of the eggs most widely used, and most readily available, including such information as size, strength of shell, color, general shape (not all eggs are egg-shaped!), and occasionally suggestions for their use. They will be divided into three categories according to size; small, medium and large.

SMALL GROUP

FINCH: Size of a small bean, bluish-white, very fragile, egg-shaped. Great for jewelry items such as earrings, pendants and stick pins. Can be cut and hinged, and even have drawers put in them! Openings may be carefully cut with cuticle scissors for diorama eggs. (Diorama eggs have one or more openings with a scene or figure inside. No hinges)

CANARY: Slightly larger than finch, blue with brown speckles, most fragile of small eggs, oval shaped. Uses as for finch. Take advantage of this egg's lovely color!

PARAKEET: About canary-sized, egg shaped, pure white, toughest-shelled of the three smallest eggs.

COCKATIEL: Diameter about the size of a nickel, white, egg-shaped, fragile. Uses as for finch, also cute done as a miniature jewel box.

DOVE: A little larger than cockatiel, white, oval shaped, slick-surfaced. Less fragile than cockatiel.

QUAIL: There are several types of quail eggs and all are popular, though the Bobwhite is the most widely used. It is white, larger than the dove, quite pointed at one end, and not too fragile. The Pharoah Quail egg is brown with darker brown specks and blotches, and larger than the Bobwhite. The Button Quail is smaller than the Bobwhite, more oval, and varied in color, but is basically brown with darker brown speckling. All may be used for a variety of things, from jewelry and miniature "bells", to jewel boxes and dioramas.

PIGEON: Diameter about the size of a quarter, waxy white, evenly rounded at both ends, very much like the dove egg. Too large for jewelry, but great for a little ring box, diorama, hinged, fancy-cut, and decoupaged.

BANTY: A small chicken egg, usually quite a bit smaller than small grocery store eggs. Color ranges from off-white to beige, and may at times be blue or greenish. Egg-shaped.

PARTRIDGE: Size of pigeon to a little larger, egg-shaped, beige with fine brown speckling.

GUINEA: Larger than partridge, cream to beige with finely pitted texture, and usually, fine light brown speckling. The very toughest of all the smaller eggs, and tougher than most larger ones, too! Very pointed. Use it for anything; great for intricate cutting, but must use a power tool to do it. A good egg for beginners learning to cut. Takes "scratch-carving" well. (Scratch carving is using any sharp instrument to scratch a design on the shell.) Color may be scrubbed or bleached away. A favorite of mine.

ARAUCANA: Another chicken egg, larger than the banty egg. Beautifully colored in blue or aqua, green, and sometimes even pink.

NOTE: Most egg shows have judged competitions for those who are exhibiting to enter if they would like. One of the categories in the judging is the Minature division. All the eggs mentioned above are suitable for that division.

General size and shape of eggs

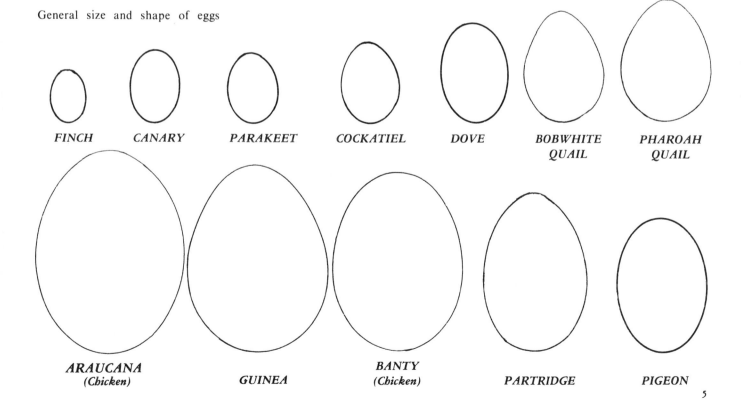

FINCH   CANARY   PARAKEET   COCKATIEL   DOVE   BOBWHITE QUAIL   PHAROAH QUAIL

ARAUCANA
(Chicken)   GUINEA   *BANTY*
(Chicken)   PARTRIDGE   PIGEON

MEDIUM GROUP:

CHICKEN: (common) This is the good old egg that everyone knows about! Size varies, and color is from white to brown. Thickness of shell will depend on where it came from. (Grocery store eggs are very thin-shelled due to the diet of the chickens, so if you can, get your eggs from a local farmer!) And no more cracking your eggs at breakfast!

DUCK: Contrary to popular belief, duck eggs are not always larger than chicken eggs, but they are considerably tougher. Shape is fairly oval; color is white or blue; texture rather waxy feeling (they won't take paint quite as well as eggs with more pourous surfaces, like goose eggs.) These eggs are a good size for Christmas ornaments, ring boxes, etc.

TURKEY: Size ranges from large duck size up. Cream colored with irregular brown speckling and may have bumpy spots on the shell. Color may be scrubbed or bleached off. Egg is quite pointed, and rather fragile for its size. It is a beautiful egg. Take advantage of its coloring.

PEACOCK: (Peacock? Everyone knows that a peacock is a boy, and can't lay eggs! Peahen is the correct term, right?) This egg is similar in size to the turkey, but in all other respects closely resembles the guinea egg. It is fairly tough-shelled. pinkish-beige in color, pointed, finely pitted, and sometimes has fine, irregular speckling. A nice egg for about any project.

GOOSE: This is probably the most popular egg for egg decorating. It is of good size, relatively tough, readily available, and affordable. Size will vary greatly, from little ones measuring under eight inches (measured around lengthwise), to those jumbo eggs which, though rare, can get to be over thirteen inches around! Generally speaking, the larger the egg is, the more elongated it will appear. (A goose just can't handle "large" and "fat" at the same time!) Also, the bigger the egg, the more fragile it is apt to be, especially at the top, or small end. When you order goose eggs, please keep in mind that not all the smaller eggs are big fat ones either! No one has yet figured out how to program geese to lay only fat eggs, and until they do, you will simply have to accept your share of the narrower ones! However, if your project requires fat eggs, most places will, for an additional charge, pick out fat ones for you. After all, they want you happy! As for the thin ones, there are many designs for which they are perfect, including Oriental vases, bells, decoupage, painting, Christmas ornaments, cutting to fit that tall, thin figure that just wouldn't look right in a fat egg, and so on.

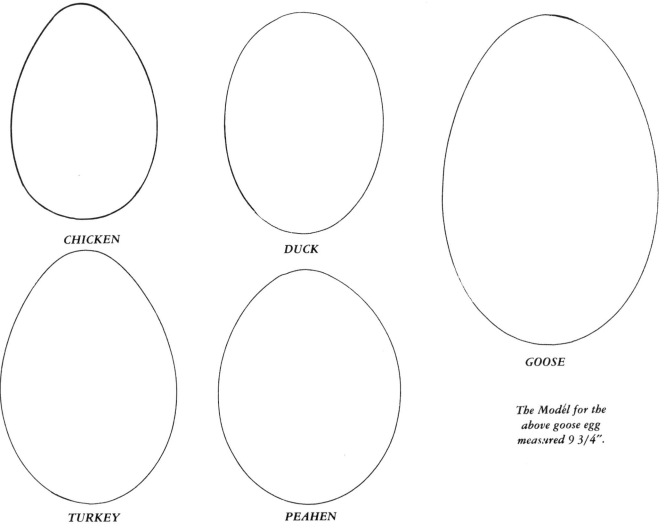

CHICKEN

DUCK

GOOSE

TURKEY

PEAHEN

The Model for the above goose egg measured 9 3/4".

LARGE GROUP:

This group consist of the ostrich family: the Rhea, Emu and African Ostrich.

RHEA:

This bird is native to South America, and looks like a miniature ostrich without some of the fancy plumage. Top weight for it is about sixty pounds. As owners of some of these birds, we have discovered something interesting about their method of parenting, Daddy does it all. I mean EVERYTHING! (Except lay the egg, of course.) The egg is off-white to butter yellow in color (the yellow is an indication that the egg is newly laid, and will eventually fade to cream or off-white.) It has a rather slick texture with fine pitting, is usually shiny and fairly thick-shelled. There is a tough membrane lining the inside of the shell (as there is with all eggs) which can be removed, leaving the shell beautifully translucent. However the membrane will lend a certain amount of strength to the shell if left intact, so for projects where it can be left, it is a good idea to do so. The shell is ususally egg-shaped, but occasionally eggs that are more oval can be found. This egg is a great favorite among eggers.

OSTRICH:

This is the largest existing bird, and lays (obviously) the largest egg. This bird is a native of Africa, and sports only two toes on each foot where the Emu and Rhea have three. (Just a little point of interest there.) Top weight for the Ostrich can be as much as three hundred pounds. Its egg is probably the most popular of all the larger eggs, partly due to the availability and moderate price, but mostly due to the fact that its great size offers so many possibilities for decorating! Its shape is quite rounded, the length and girth measurements occasionally being within a half-inch of each other! This feature allows ample space inside for almost any project imaginable, and makes it one of my all-time favorite eggs. (Some people feel that this same feature actually detracts from the egg because it loses the "egg" look. However, this has never been a problem for me, because it is, after all, an egg!)

Top size for this egg has been known to reach twenty inches, though this is very large. An average size range is from sixteen to eighteen inches, with larger and smaller sizes usually available. The thickness of the shell is almost 1/8", making it very durable. The color is off-white to cream, texture is pitted, and surface may be shiny or dull, but is most often shiny. Emu and Rhea eggs are usually obtained from sources within the USA, but most Ostrich eggs are shipped from Africa. They nearly always have only one emptying hole (which is usually irregular in shape and off-centered).

EMU: Native of Australia, this bird weighs in at about ninety pounds. It is a little darker in color than the Rhea and doesn't resemble the African Ostrich quite so much. Its egg doesn't resemble the African Ostrich egg in any way at all. In size it is much like the Rhea egg, but is more oval. The striking thing about this egg is its color. At first glance it appears to be black, but on closer examination, an underlying color of aqua or gray may be seen in the pitting of the shell. Scratch through the black outer layer, and you have this lovely contrasting color showing through! The aqua color will eventually turn more gray, though spraying with a fixative may retard the fading process somewhat. Decorations on the outside of this egg should complement its unusual color and play it up! This egg is the most costly of the eggs mentioned.

All three of the larger eggs offer untold possibilities for decorating, and once you have gotten the "feel" of working with eggs, you will surely want to invest in the tools and start working with these bigger ones! A few of the things that may be done include musical eggs, lamps, display cabinets to hold your favorite keepsakes (or even your tiny eggs), purses, jewel boxes, clocks, eggs commemorating special occasions, and ones with miniature lighting in them. The list goes on and on!

Now that you know about the eggs themselves, you will need to know what tools to have in order to do something with them!

CHAPTER IV ❧ TOOLS

There is a large variety of tools used by eggers, some of which may be purchased from craft, hobby, or hardware stores. However, you will probably find it necessary to purchase many of your supplies from mail order businesses specializing in egg supplies.

In getting started, you won't be needing any specialized or expensive tools. Most of the projects in this book call for tools which can be readily found around the house or purchased at local stores, with little investment involved.

The Beginner's Tool Kit Should Have The Following:
(See Plates One & Three)

1. SCISSORS, manicure or decoupage: These are tiny scissors with thin, curved blades and sharp points. Use for cutting eggs, prints, braids, etc.

2. SCISSORS, larger scissors: for cutting paper, cardboard, fabric.

3. TWEEZERS: A couple of pairs of tweezers are handy. One should be fairly long, at least 4", and have curved tips for reaching into tight places. Use them for placing or arranging things on the inside or outside of eggs.

4. DRAPE STICK: A handle of wood or metal with a heavy pin at one end. Use this for arranging fabric and other items, applying glue, etc.

5. PLIERS: Small needle-nose or fine-point pliers are ideal for bending hinges, findings, and wires to desired shapes. Two pairs are best, one to hold an object, the other to bend or shape it.

6. BRUSHES: Several brushes of varying sizes are useful. Use flat brushes for applying finishes; round brushes for decorative painting. Soft bristles are best, except when applying pastelling chalks, where a stiff-bristled brush works the best. (An old worn-out brush is ideal).

7. EGG HOLDERS: These hold the egg, either while you are working on it, or while something done to the egg is drying. Two styles are available commercially, the skewer-type and the spring-type. The skewer-type is a metal rod with a handle at one end and two rubber stoppers to hold the egg. A simple home-made one can be made from a knitting needle and two rubber bands. Simply pass the knitting needle through the egg and wind the rubber bands around the needle at each end of the egg, securing it in place. The commercial holders come with a stand to put the rods in, but you can prop yours in a glass or other object which will hold it upright.

The spring-type is different. It is a wooden handle having three long, curving wires at one end. The wires are held together in a "closed" position by a bead or other object, while the ends of the wires are passed through one hole in the egg. Then the bead is pulled back toward the handle, allowing the wires to expand against the inside of the egg. This is an ideal way to hold eggs which are going to be dipped in a finish, and about the only way to hold an egg with only one hole.

8. MISCELLANEOUS: These are the common items every tool box should have: pencils, erasers, measuring tape, ruler, rubber bands, and paper towels. I use part of a foam rubber cushion with a cupped place cut out to hold the egg.

9. LIGHT: This pretty well speaks for itself. Good lighting is a must.

As you progress, you will want to add to your tool box anything which will make your egging easier, faster, and more fun. The following items will help: *(See Plates 2 & 3).*

1. GLUE DISPENSERS: These are syringes with long tips, used for putting glue in hard-to-reach places, or places which call for a thin line of glue. Just fill the dispenser with the glue you want to use (a white glue), and start gluing! The tip may be heated and reshaped for specific applications.

2. GLUE TIPS: An alternative to the glue dispenser. These fit, or can be cut to fit most glue bottles. By cutting the tip to the desired size, you can control the amount of glue that is dispensed. These, too, may be heated and reshaped.

3. SPONGE APPLICATORS: Use these in place of brushes for applying finishes. They eliminate brush marks.

4. FLOWER TOOLS: Wooden tools used for "raised decoupage" (also known as paper tole or bas relief), and for shaping bread dough, or modeling compounds.

5. NEEDLE FILES: Miniature files in different shapes, used for smoothing edges, enlarging holes, shaping, etc.

6. ROUND-NOSE or ROSARY PLIERS: Pliers with rounded tips, used for shaping wires and findings.

7. DIAGONAL CUTTING PLIERS: Used for cutting wire and other metal objects. (This Fig. 7 applies only to Plate 2! The Fig. 7 in Plate 3 is an egg holder.)

8. EGG BLOWER: Replaces lung-power, so is a must for anyone who is blowing out very many eggs! It is inexpensive and easy to use. Directions come with it.

9. TEMPLATES: Templates are great for marking circles or ovals on eggs, or other objects. You will find them useful for making "floors" for inside your eggs, for instance.

10. EGG MARKER: There are several good egg markers available, and they are well worth the investment! It is one tool which I feel is a must if you are serious about egging at all. If you have tried marking your eggs with rubber bands, etc., you will know what I mean. The egg marker will take all the guesswork and tedium out of marking, and will open up a whole new

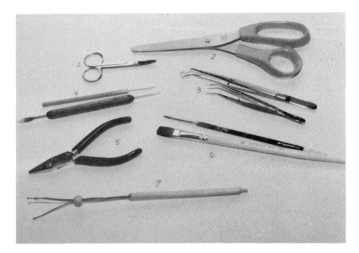

PLATE 1: Beginner's Tools

world for you. You will be marking eggs you would never have attempted before, and marking simple eggs faster and more accurately. It may take a little time to learn to use your marker, but once you do, you will enjoy it thoroughly!

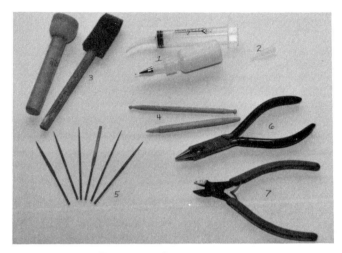

PLATE 2: Miscellaneous Tools

11. ELECTRIC CUTTING TOOLS: These are small, hand-held power tools used for cutting eggs. They should have at least 30,000 RPM. (The vibration of slower tools tends to have a shattering effect on eggs.) One of the most popular of the tools is the Dremel, for which a large number of cutting and grinding tools are available. Several of these are useful for egg decorating, as listed below: *(See Plate 4).*

A. Emery Cutting Wheel: This is a 7/8″ disc, used with a mandrel and 1/8″ collet. (A mandrel is a small rod which holds this disc; and the collet holds the mandrel in place in the Dremel. Correct collet size will be listed with each tool.) Use the emery wheel for making straight, or very slightly curved cuts, (its size prevents it from being used for the more intricate cutting). It will cut most eggs, but will wear down, or break, and need to be replaced.

B. Silicon Grinding Points: These come in a variety of shapes and sizes. The cone-shaped points are useful for drilling holes in the ends of eggs, and for smoothing edges on eggs, filigrees, etc. Uses 3/32″ collet.

C. Carbide Bur: A dental drill, very good for cutting intricate designs; comes in different sizes. The tiny, thin ones break rather easily, so handle with care. May be used in the Dremel with a 1/16″ collet, or in the dental tools which are becoming so popular. Purchase these from egg supply or dental supply houses.

D. Diamond Cutters: Available only through egg decorating or dental supply houses. The surface of these cutters is too rough and too thick for use with the smaller, more fragile eggs, but is ideal for cutting the tougher eggs, especially those of the ostrich family. The small diameter of the cutters allows you to cut fairly tight curves. This is one of the cutters I use most often.

It is rather expensive, but lasts a long time. They are available in two shaft sizes, the larger using a 3/32″ collet, the smaller using a 1/16″ collet. The smaller one will also fit the dental drill.

F. Flame Drill: A small, pointed (flame-shaped) diamond cutter. Use this for doing intricate cutting, as you would the carbide bur. It will cut a wider swath than the carbide bur, but will not break as easily. I use it often for drilling eyelet holes for hinges. It takes a 1/16″ collet, and may be used in the dental drill. Purchase from egg or dental supply.

12. DENTAL DRILLS: (also known as air drills) These have recently emerged as an exciting new way to cut eggs! Their extremely high RPM (400,000!) lets you cut a fragile egg with ease because there is so little vibration. The hand-piece is small, easily held, and weighs almost nothing. There are some drawbacks to them, however, the main one being the cost. (The hand piece is rather expensive, and requires an air compressor to run it). Also, they bog down under load, so do not cut the larger egges very well. The bits used in the dental drill may be purchased from egg supply or dental supply houses, or you might ask your dentist to save burs for you. Dental drill burs may be used in the Dremel, using a 1/16″ collet.

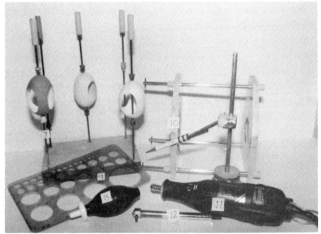

PLATE 3: Electric & Misc. Tools

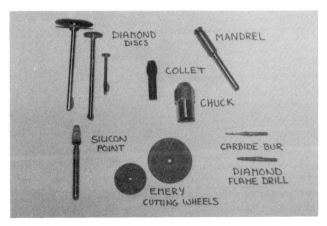

PLATE 4: Cutting Supplies

9

CHAPTER V ❧ GLUES AND DECORATIVE FINISHES

No tool box is complete without the necessary adhesives and finishes. There are many of each to choose from, and you will soon find the ones that work the best for you, and give the results you are looking for.

Always be neat with your glues and finishes! A sloppy job can ruin an otherwise perfect egg. Moist towelettes, used for babies, and easily found at any drug or grocery store, are great for minor clean-ups.

GLUES

There are three main adhesives used by eggers: epoxy, cement, and the "white" glues.

1. EPOXY: This is a two-part adhesive which must be mixed. The 5-minute type is best, since its fast set-up time allows you to proceed on your project quickly. This glue is ideal for anything that will have stress, such as gluing metal bases to eggs or to onyx, applying hinges, and making repairs. Use it anywhere that you will want a super hold.

Work quickly when using epoxy. Have everything ready to be glued before you mix it, otherwise it will be hardening before you get a chance to use it. Don't use it once it gets stiff and stringy, because it won't hold. (You can mix it until it becomes somewhat tacky, so it will hold right away, but you must put your pieces together exactly as you want them on the first try, because it isn't likely that you will have much time to move them after that.)

Epoxy comes in tubes, dual dispensers (which look like two attached syringes), and plastic squeeze bottles. I like the squeeze bottles the best.

A useful idea, developed by Aline Becker, is to mix a small amount of shredded paper towel with epoxy to give bulk. This way it will fill a hollow place between egg and stand, stand and onyx, etc. When putting music boxes in eggs, pack this mixture around them, and you will never have to worry about the music box coming loose when the key is wound!

If you need to unglue something that has been epoxied, see the "Trouble-Shooting" section of this book.

2. CEMENTS: These are glues, used about the same way epoxy is used, that don't require mixing. I have not found them to be as useful as epoxy because they take longer to set up, and I don't feel that they hold quite as well.

3. WHITE GLUES: As the name indicates, these glues are white in color, though they dry clear. The thin white glues, such as Elmer's are great for such things as gluing large areas of beads. Its thinness allows ample time for working with the beads before they set up. It is also useful for applying prints or sprinkle-on finishes, such as pearl flakes, glitter, etc.

The "tacky" glues are thicker, and are used where quicker hold is needed. They are thick enough to hold almost anything in place, including heavy fabrics, braids, and other trims, and won't soak through velvet, unless you put on more than you need. Don't try to use this, or any water-base glue, in place of epoxy. It might hold for a while, but you will have problems with it sooner or later.

The paste-type glues, such as Velverette, are useful in places where even tacky isn't stiff enough to hold. Tacky glue is thin enough to use in a squeeze bottle, but these glues must be applied with a drape stick or other tool.

4. MISCELLANEOUS: In addition to the three main types of glues, there are some whose uses are limited, but which are perfect for certain jobs. One of these is the silicon adhesive. It is a glue which will hold its shape when squeezed from the tube, and becomes rubbery when dry. However, it is not a thick glue, and won't hold an object if it has any weight to it at all. I have used it for holding such things as silk, paper, or dried flowers, or anything very lightweight which I want to be slightly elevated. I have seen it used to make "waves" in an egg with an ocean scene. Painted to look like waves, it was very realistic! This glue, or sealant, comes in clear or white, and is available from hardware and department stores. It takes a day or so to dry, so be patient with it.

DECORATIVE FINISHES

There is a wide variety of finishes, and you will want to experiment with all of them! Each can produce widely varied and lovely effects. Following is information about some of the more commonly used finishes.

1. PAINTS: Almost any kind of paint may be used on eggs, including watercolor, oils and acrylics. Paints used in ceramics, (the kind that do not need to be fired!) are one of the best types for use with eggs. They go on smoothly, have good color, and cover with the fewest number of coats. Also, they are readily available in most locations, and reasonably priced.

Use your imagination when painting an egg. Lovely and unusual effects may be had from such paints as model car paints. Put a few colors of these nonwater-base paints in a cup of water, swirl slightly, and dip an egg in it. When you take the egg out, it will have a very interesting marbleized pattern on it. (Slowly turn the egg until the paint has completely set up, or it will run to the bottom and drip off, or form a blob).

2. ANTIQUING STAINS: These may be used to antique findings, stands, etc. They are available in both water-base and nonwater-base. You will need a solvent for the nonwater-base variety.

3. SEALERS: A sealer is a must. Too often I have put a finish over my beautifully painted egg only to have the lovely color change before my eyes! A sealer over the paint would have prevented this. I like to use Glosseal over acrylic paints. It is water-based, has no odor, and is easy to clean up. In the jar, it looks like Elmer's glue, but will dry clear and shiny. It can be used as a finish as well as a sealer.

There are nonwater-base sealers, too, if you prefer. Many of them have specific applications, like for wood or gold leaf, but you should be able to use them in other areas as well.

4. CLEAR FINISHES: These are any liquid finishes, water-base or nonwater-base, which will be the final finish on an egg. They may be high gloss, satin, or matte (also called "bisque" which means it has no shine at all).

The water-base finishes include such products a Regal Egg Sheen, Mod Podge, and other similar products, of which there are many. They are milky white in the jar, but dry clear. They may be used as the final finish on your egg, or used to "build up" coats in preparation for a different product to be used over them. I do this often when decoupaging an egg. These finishes may be wet-sanded to produce a smooth finish with no brush marks. Many of them may be used to "lift a print", which means to take the colored portion of a print off the paper it is mounted on. It is then a decal, of sorts, and is quite flexible with its plastic-like coating. Directions for this are usually on the label.

Nonwater-base finishes will add beauty and protection to your eggs. They are waterproof, and will take handling quite well. Multiple coats, brushed over raised decoupage, harden the paper and give it a porcelainized look. Regular decoupaged eggs may be dipped any number of times to properly "sink" a print, and produce a perfect finish with no brush marks.

Glostique and Deep Flex are among the most widely used of the nonwater-base finishes. (Be sure to use these, and other nonwater-base finishes, in well ventilated areas. This cannot be stressed enough!) Usually there is a choice between matte (bisque) and gloss, and you may also have a choice between brushing it on or spraying it on. The two products mentioned above need their own type of thinner for clean-up; be sure to get some when you get the finish. Nothing else will work on them, although these two thinners will work interchangeably.

For fun, you might try this; dip a filigree finding in Glostique until the holes are filled. When it is dry, color the Glostique with glass stain or colored marking pens. The effect is beautiful!

Using these products directly over paint must be done with caution, since they can cause bleeding or changing of colors. It is very disappointing to have your egg change colors just when you think you are putting on the final touches! So, use a sealer over your paint before using one of these finishes. Finally, be absolutely sure that the surface you are about to apply one of these products to is throughly dry. These products are waterproof and will hold moisture in as well as out, and this will eventually cause problems, such as dulling and crazing.

5. DECAL-IT and CRACKLE-IT: For making decals out of prints (lifting a print), Decal-It is the product I prefer. It makes a tough decal, which will take a lot of handling and manipulating while being put on an egg. (The use of this product will be explained more fully in Chapter XI.)
Crackle-It is a companion product which produces an antique "crazed" look. This product will not work without Decal-It, so if you want your egg to have a crackle finish, you will have to get both products. The directions on the bottle recommend letting it dry for forty-eight hours before antiquing it. This is to give the "crackles" time to form. I have done this, only to find a week later that many more crackles had formed! So I recommend that you let it dry at least five to seven days before antiquing it.

6. VARNISHES: Liquitex Matte Varnish is a favorite of many eggers. It is water-base and gives a satin sheen when dry. It works very well on wood, giving it a waxed look. It may also be used to lift a print.

7. GLASS STAINS: These can be fun to work with. They are available both water-base and nonwater-base. Use them for coloring light bulbs for miniature lighting, or for coloring clear plastic for a "stained-glass" look. As mentioned above, it can be used to color findings which have been dipped in Glostique. Also, you can mix the nonwater-base type with epoxy for making ponds, streams, etc.

8. POWDERS: These are available in several colors, plus mother-of-pearl, and irridescent. They act as a buffing compound, so will add more shine to a glossy surface. (They must be used over a glossy finish, such as Glostique.) Watch out for finger prints after using any of these products. Handle your egg with a soft cloth. You may put a coat of finish over them, but it will dull the shine, defeating your purpose.

9. GOLD LEAF: Gold leafing takes some time to do, but the results are worth it! Gold paint, no matter how good, just can't compare. Gold leaf is very thin and takes careful handling, so you will want to work in a place where there is no moving air (I even hold my breath part of the time!) Actually, it is not hard to do, though. The adhesive used for gold leafing stays tacky for quite a long time, allowing ample time to apply the leaf. Handle the leaf with tweezers, not your fingers, as the oils in your skin will cause it to tarnish. Be sure to use a gold leaf sealer over it after the adhesive is thoroughly dry.

Gold leaf kits are available and contain everything you will need, including complete instructions.

10. CERAMIC PASTEL CHALKS: These are colored chalks especially formulated for use with ceramics. They differ from artist's pastels in that they have a binding agent which helps them stick to the piece to which they are applied. They are ideal for eggs and have many applications. They may be used in conjunction with paints, either to highlight or give shadow. Use them on painted or unpainted figurines, stands, eggs, etc. They are especially nice for adding color to facial features on figurines, such as coloring lips and rouging cheeks. Use them to alter colors in prints, and to shade around flowers and leaves on decoupaged or raised-decoupaged eggs. The uses are limitless! This is one of my favorite products.

To help the chalk stick even better, coat the objects to be colored with Regal Egg Sheen first. It will ensure a good bond, but will still allow you to wash off any mistakes.

11. SPRINKLE-ON FINISHES: This group includes such products as glitter, diamond dust, pearl flakes and ballentine. Everyone knows what glitter is, but the others might need a little explaining.

Diamond dust is similiar to glitter in shape and texture, but has no real color. It appears white in the container, but when put over a print, the print is visible through it. It has a nice sparkle, making it good for simulated snow. I use it frequently on Christmas eggs.

Pearl flakes are just that, little flakes of mother-of-pearl. They are presently available only in white, but may be dyed any desired color, or colored with ceramic chalks after they have been put on an egg. (The chalk doesn't really color the flakes, but clings in the spaces and cracks between them, giving a beautiful finish.) If they are sprinkled very lightly over paint, the paint will show through. Coat pearl flakes with a clear finish, preferably nonwater-base, to protect them. (Water-base finishes tend to dull pearl flakes somewhat).

Ballentine is tiny glass beads, almost too small to see. In bulk, they have a pale-gray color, but appear clear when put on an egg. They have very little sparkle, but will give decoupaged eggs an interesting "three-dimensional" appearance.

All the sprinkle-on finishes mentioned (which are only a few of the ones available!) are applied basically the same way. Coat all, or a portion, of the egg with one of the white glues, spreading it on as evenly as possible. (I usually use tacky.) Quickly sprinkle or pour the product on, covering the glued area as thoroughly as possible. (A second sprinkling won't hurt). Do this over a container, which will catch the surplus for reuse. When the egg is covered, prop it up where it can dry without touching anything. (This is a good place to use an egg holder!)

I apply pearl flakes a little differently. Usually the flakes are a bit bigger than I like, so I break them up before applying them. The other products can be poured on using a spoon or even a shaker jar, but I like to apply pearl flakes by hand, a pinch at a time. This way I can spread them out thinly so the color of the egg or paint below will show through.

There are many products besides the ones mentioned here, and there is no end to the different "looks" your eggs can have through the inventive use of them. Don't be afraid to experiment with something new! This is what makes egg decorating so unique and so challenging! If something unexpected happens, and it often does, you have either learned what not to do, or you may have developed a new technique that will be very useful.

CHAPTER VI ❧ EMPTYING THE EGG

There are three basic ways to empty an egg. You can blow it, cut it, or break it. For obvious reasons, I will only be discussing the first two.

Here are a few things to keep in mind as you begin to empty your first egg. Make sure your egg is shaped right, free of cracks and blemishes, and uncooked. If your egg needs to be cleaned, scrub it with cleanser. Bleach is occasionally the only way to get some stains off, but too much bleach will weaken, or even destroy, the shell. Do not use anything oily on the shell. An oily residue will prevent any finish you put on from sticking. Don't worry about discoloration if the egg is to be painted later.

Many eggs are available already blown and cleaned. With a few exceptions, they will have two holes, one at each end, just like the eggs you will be emptying.

METHOD ONE — BLOWING:

1) Tools and Supplies Needed.

A. Of course you need the egg!

B. A tool to make the holes. This may be anything from a needle for a tiny egg to a small nail for an egg up to goose size. You will find the tool that you are most comfortable and successful with. (If you have an electric tool, use a cone shaped bit in it to make the holes).

C. A tool to stir the yolk with, such as a straightened paper clip.

D. A container to catch the egg. (Save the egg for eating or cooking!)

E. If you have an Egg Blower, by all means use it! (See tool section.)

2) Technique For Blowing.

A. Gently puncture holes in each end of the egg. The top hole (usually at the small end of the egg) may be no bigger than the object used to make it. This is the hole you will be blowing through. Make the bottom hole somewhat larger so the egg can freely pass through it. It won't ever need to be larger than one-fourth inch. Be sure the holes are well centered, and as neat as possible. (If you have trouble getting your holes in the center, a piece of carbon paper will help. Put the carbon paper on a flat surface, hold the egg above it, as straight up-and-down as possible, and touch it to the carbon paper. This will give you a well-centered mark to go by.)

B. Using a straightened paper clip, stir the yolk inside the egg. This breaks the sac the yolk is in and alows it to go through the hole easier. (The yolk will usually break on its own, but stirring won't hurt!)

C. Now you can apply some lung power to the small hole! Blow until the entire contents of the egg are in the bowl. If you are having a hard time getting the egg out, check to make sure your holes are large enough, and that they are free of membrane. (There is a membrane which lines the inside of all eggs, and sometimes it will block the hole.)

D. If you have the bulb-type egg blower, use it, following the directions that come with it. If you empty very many eggs, you will certainly want to invest a few dollars to get one!

E. Now that your egg is empty, clean the inside of any residue by running some water in it. (You don't need to fill it, just put in enough to slosh around.) After sloshing, blow it out. Repeat this until you are sure that there is no egg residue left inside. Give it a final rinsing with a disinfectant solution to prevent odor and discourage bugs. (You can use a syringe to put water in the egg instead of running it under the tap. A large syringe from the drug store will do nicely.)

F. When the egg is cleaned, set it on end on a paper towel to drain. Be sure one hole is straight down and in contact with the paper towel. (The paper towel will act as a wick, and draw the water out.)

METHOD TWO — CUTTING:

With this method there is no blowing to do. You start with a whole egg and, in one neat step, you have a shell to decorate and an egg to fry! Due to their thickness, some eggs are not as easy to cut as others, but generally speaking, you should be able to cut any egg up to and including goose eggs.

1) Tools and Supplies Needed.
    A. The egg.
    B. Manicure scissors, or some of similar size, with curved blades.
    C. Pencil.
    D. Power tool, (instead of scissors) with carbide cutter or flame drill.
    E. Clear nail polish. (This is optional.)
2) Techinique For Cutting.
    A. With the pencil, draw an oval on the shell, making the size and shape of the oval suit the size and shape of the shell. (Fig. 1-A).
    B. Put a coating of clear nail polish over the oval (cutting line). This will help strengthen the shell where you will be cutting, and will keep the cut edge from being so ragged. This is an optional step, but a good idea if you are using thin-shelled eggs. Egg Sheen or a similiar product may also be used.
    C. Using the point of your cuticle scissors, puncture a hole inside the oval. Be sure not to twist the blade in the hole, or you will probably end up with a broken egg! (Fig. 1-B).

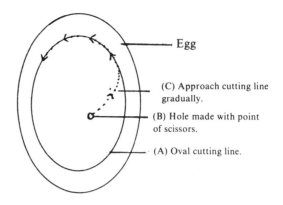

(C) Approach cutting line gradually.

(B) Hole made with point of scissors.

(A) Oval cutting line.

Fig. 1

D. Using this hole as a starting point, begin cutting, gradually working your way to the cutting line. Be sure to hold your scissors so that the curve of the blade goes with the curve of the oval. If you are right-handed, you will be cutting in a counter-clockwise direction. Always make small cuts, using the middle part of the blades, and never make sharp turns. Approach the cutting line by cutting in a curve (Fig. 1-C).

E. When you have cut all the way around, lift off the piece of shell, and pour the contents of the egg into the container.

F. Clean the inside of the egg, using a disinfectant,. Remove any loose membrane, but leave any which is intact, since it adds strength to the shell. Put the egg, hole-side down, on a paper towel to dry.

When using a Dremel or other power tool to empty an egg, be sure to use a carbide cutter or flame drill, rather than a disc, because a disc will throw raw egg everywhere! A flame drill or carbide cutter cuts differently, and won't do that.

CHAPTER VII ❧ MARKING THE EGG

The markings you put on your egg will form the foundation for everything else you will do to it, so it only makes sense to say that you need to do the best possible job on this part. Some designs will require very simple markings, only a line or two being sufficient. Other projects may involve precision marking, requiring equipment and considerable time.

A few bits of information to help you create a nicer egg are in order here. First, when you have chosen the design you want to do, match the egg to it; or conversely, if you have an egg you want to use, match the design to the egg. Some eggs are short and fat, while others are long and slender. If you have a figurine which is tall and thin, you wouldn't choose a short, fat egg to put it in. Obviously, it would look better in an egg that is also long and slender.

The same thing applies to any markings you put on the egg, whether they will be for cutting lines, or for patterns to be followed in decorating. Either way, the lines you apply should be appropriate and complimentary to the size and shape of the egg.

Since the lines you put on the egg will form the basis of your entire design, be sure they are straight! If your first line is put on crooked, your entire design will be crooked. Get used to "eyeing" your egg often to detect any crooked lines and straighten them up! Don't use the end-holes as a guide - they are rarely centered!

If you will be cutting with scissors, keep in mind that the variety of designs you can cut will be limited by the fact that scissors will not make a smooth cut edge. One side may be fairly smooth, but the other will be rough. For this reason, you will be unable to cut projects which call for edges that will meet, such as a jewel box. Stick to designs where the piece which is cut away can be discarded or trimmed and used for another project.

Use your imagination when marking your eggs. For instance, you can make a simple jewel box by marking a straight line around an egg, but you can add interest to it by giving that straight line a little curve in the front. (Fig. 2).

Fig. 2

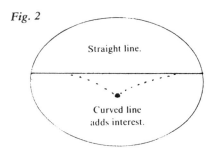

Straight line.

Curved line adds interest.

Now to the different ways to mark eggs:

FREEHAND: It is important that you develop the ability to do some freehand marking. This doesn't mean that you should be able to do the entire design freehand. There's no point, since there are other means of doing the bulk of the marking faster, easier and more accurately. But there are some parts of designs that can only be done freehand, and you should be able to do them. Practice is the only way to learn this. If it doesn't look right, erase it and do it again!

RUBBER BAND: A wide (1/4" or so) rubber band can be stretched around the egg and used as a straight-edge to mark against. I did this for years before I got my first egg marker. It takes considerable time, because it is very hard to get the rubber band straight on the egg! If if looks straight from one angle, it will look crooked from another. Straighten it there, and it looks crooked somewhere else! And on and on ...But it *will* work if you keep at it. Another problem is this: you want to mark your egg around the middle, so you put your rubber band

on. But now the rubber band is in the middle of the egg where your pencil mark should go. So you move the rubber band to one side a little. Now it doesn't look right at all, because one side of the egg looks big and the other small. Well, you see the problem, so let me say this: a rubber band is all right only if you absolutely do not have another choice!

PAPER STRIPS: A strip of paper, about a half-inch wide, and as long as the distance around your egg, can be very handy, sometimes even more so than a tape measure. For instance, lets say you want to divide your egg into eight equal divisions and you are using a goose egg measuring nine and seven-eighths inches. It would take considerable time to figure that out with a tape measure (at least, it would for me!). Instead, just take your little strip of paper, which measures nine and seven-eights inches, the same as your egg, and fold it in half. Fold it in half two more times. When you open it out, your fold marks represent eight perfectly spaced divisions! Of course you will have to count the ends where they meet around your egg as one division, but isn't that simple? I also use strips of paper as a straight-edge to mark against when it cannot be done with the egg-marker.

TEMPLATES: Plastic circle and oval templates are very useful tools . For some reason, the templates with the right sized ovals are not as easy to come by as the ones with circles, so if you come across one somewhere, better grab it. Use them for making doors or other openings in eggs, and for making circles for floors.

EGG-MARKERS: If you are serious about egging, they are well worth the investment! There are several good ones on the market, each with a full set of instructions. See the Tool and Projects Chapters for more information.

Each project in the back of the book will give detailed instructions for marking specific designs on eggs. You will get experience using several different methods. From these, you should be able to do variations of your own.

CHAPTER VIII ❧ *CUTTING*

Fig. 3

First a word of caution: EGG DUST IS VERY HARMFUL TO BREATHE! If you are cutting with a power tool of any kind, you need to protect your lungs from the dust. Wear a mask! And wear goggles to protect your eyes!

An alternative to masks and goggles is a cutting box, which I have found to be very helpful. Mine is made of plywood and plexiglass, with arm-holes in the front to work through, and a hole at the side for the hose of a vacuum cleaner to fit through. The end of the hose is close to where I do my cutting, and picks up most of the dust. Another benefit, besides keeping dust and particles out of eyes and lungs, is that it also keeps it out of the rest of the building where you are working! See Fig. 3 for dimensions on cutting box. You may adjust dimensions to suit your own needs.

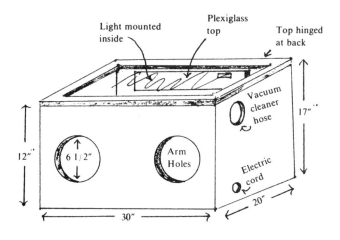

Light mounted inside

Plexiglass top

Top hinged at back

Vacuum cleaner hose

Electric cord

17"

12"

6 1/2"

Arm Holes

30"

20"

Now, down to business . . . There are several ways to cut an egg besides using cuticle scissors, which you have already read about in the chapter on Emptying Eggs. Two of these methods are old, and seldom used now, so I will just gloss over them.

1. RAZOR BLADE: A tedious and time consuming method, especially on the larger eggs, but perseverance will get the job done! The designs you can do are limited because it is hard to cut a curve with a razor blade. Be sure to use a single-edge blade!

2. COPING SAW: (jeweler's saw) Another hard way to do it, but not quite as hard as with the razor blade. Again, design is limited.

The following methods are the easiest and most fun, but require the purchase of the proper tools.

1. ELECTRIC CUTTING TOOL: (This may be any power tool which produces a high enough RPM. A Dremel Moto Tool is a good example.)

If you are going to be cutting a chicken egg jewel box, for instance, select a *cutting disc,* such as the emery cutting wheel, to use. *(Plate 4, Page 9).* Once you are ready to cut, grasp the tool in your hand with your fingers close to the nut that holds the collet in place. The bulk of the tool will be in the palm of your hand. (The farther back you hold the tool, the less control you will have, so stay as close to the front as possible without getting tangled up in moving parts!) Holding it where the air holes are is all right, just don't block them off. Have something to rest your hand or wrist on while cutting. I rest my hand on an empty egg carton inside the cutting box, while the hand holding the egg is resting either on the egg carton or on the floor of the cutting box, depending on the size of the egg I am cutting. You will develop a method that is right for you. Just keep in mind that proper support for both hands is very important for a well-controlled, steady cut.

Holding the egg firmly in your hand, put the disc to the cutting line using slow, gentle pressure. Let the tool do the work. As soon as the disc has penetrated the shell, begin to move the tool or the egg, or both, so that the disc will be cutting along the line. Don't hold the disc in the same place for any length of time, or it will make a wider cut than you want, and may scorch the egg a little where it makes contact. Continue turning the egg, withdrawing the disc to adjust positions as needed, until you have cut all the way around.

Fig. 4

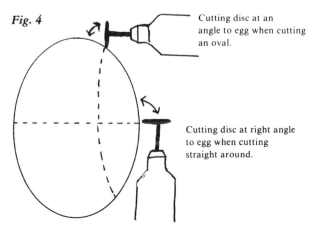

Cutting disc at an angle to egg when cutting an oval.

Cutting disc at right angle to egg when cutting straight around.

To cut straight around the egg, you hold the disc straight up and down against the cutting line, and it works perfectly. But if you want to make an oval door in the front of the egg, you will have a hard time doing it by holding the disc this way. The reason is that the width of the disc would prevent you from cutting in a tight circle without producing gouged places in the cutting line. The way to get around this is to hold the disc against the cutting line at an angle, rather than straight-on. Try it. A little practice will show you what I mean. *(Fig. 4)*

Another thing that will help cut an oval is to use one of the diamond cutting discs which have a smaller diameter. You will still cut at an angle, but it won't need to be quite so exaggerated. Another alternative is to use a carbide cutter or flame drill. These are fine, if all you want is an opening without a door. A flame drill cuts a swath too wide for making a good hinged door. The carbide cutter takes a very steady hand. Every tiny movement of the hand will show up in the cut! To a somewhat lesser degree, this is also true of the flame drill.

You will soon learn which tools to use for which jobs, and you will develop your own favorites. For a hinged cut, or a straight cut not to be hinged, I will almost always use a diamond cutting disc. For filigree cuts or other cuts not to be hinged, I will usually use the flame drill or carbide cutter.

When using a *flame drill* or *carbide cutter,* hold the Dremel like a pencil, keeping your hand close to the front of the tool. Remember to support both hands while cutting. Put gentle pressure against the egg somewhere on the cutting line. The drill should be aimed **STRAIGHT** at the egg, not at an angle. If you put pressure on the drill from an angle, you may break your bur or flame drill. especially if you are cutting one of the larger eggs. Once the drill has penetrated the shell, gently follow the outline of your design, withdrawing the drill and turning the egg as needed. Again, let the drill do the work. Don't rush it.

2. DENTAL DRILL: (also known as Air Tool or Air Drill) This is the high-speed drill which has revolutionized egg cutting! It is used very much like the Dremel, but you will notice a completely different "feel" to it. The hand-piece is almost as small as a pencil and very lightweight, making it easy to handle. The drill is "air driven," meaning it needs an air compressor to run, and the sound of it will produce fond memories of your favorite dentist. . . . .

On the smaller eggs, under goose size, it cuts like a dream. It will cut a filigree pattern so fine you will wonder what is holding the egg together, and does it with the ease of drawing with a pencil! The techniques of cutting with it are just the same as with the Dremel; hold it pencil-style for cutting with burs or flame drills, and in the palm of the hand for cutting with discs.

At first, you may be a little hesitant and nervous about cutting, but just give it a try! Like anything new, it takes a little getting used to. In a short time you will be cutting like a pro! And don't worry about the eggs that didn't quite make it through the training period. Most can be used for something, even if it isn't for what they were originally intended.

If you are not ready to make the investment in a cutting tool, but would like to decorate some of the fancier cut eggs, there are pre-cut eggs available from several egg supply mail-order houses. You can choose from what they have available or ask for your own design to be cut. However, sooner or later, you will be ready for the challenge of doing your own cutting.

For more information about cutting, see the projects at the back of the book. There you will find complete instructions for doing all the basic cuts.

CHAPTER IX   HINGING

There are several ways to apply hinges. Which method you use will be determined by what results you want from the hinging, the size of the egg and/or the hinged part, and by what is or isn't available to you.

Hinges come in different sizes. The largest ones, used on ostrich eggs, range from about 5/8 to 3/4" wide. Some hinges have holes in them, which I prefer because glue collects in the holes, giving the hinge that much more grip. See *Plate 5* for some of the hinges available.

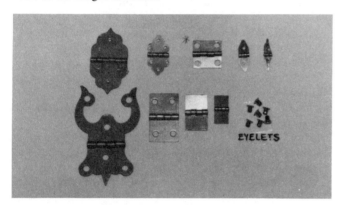

PLATE 5: Shown actual size.

THE RIGHT HINGE:

When getting ready to hinge an egg, you must choose a hinge that is correct for the size of the egg. The hinges shown in *Plate 5* might help you decide. My favorite hinge, the starred one, can be used on eggs ranging in size from duck to ostrich, and I like it because I have the option of putting eyelets in the holes if I feel the egg needs it. I will explain this more fully later.

WHICH TECHNIQUE?:

Lets assume that you have a goose egg, marked for a simple jewel box, ready to hinge. You have chosen the "starred" hinge, but you cannot glue it on without making some kind of cut first. (If you did put it on without making a cut, you would not be able to open the egg, because there would be no way to cut the part under the hinge). You have two choices: one is to cut only the hinge area, and the other is to cut all the way around the egg. around the egg.

Here are the advantages and disadvantages of both: If you cut only the hinge area, you can attach the entire hinge at one time, which is quick and easy to do, but you have to contend with half of the egg flopping around on the hinge while you are trying to work on the other half. Obviously, this could be a problem.

The other choice is to cut the egg in half and attach half the hinge at a time. This makes decorating the egg easier because you are able to work on the pieces separately. The drawback is that, after being decorated, the two halves may not fit back together properly. When you are working on an egg that is hinged together, you automatically close it periodically to check for proper fit, but when you are working with two separate pieces, it is easy to forget to do this. If you do forget, the lining and trims you put on will almost always prevent proper closing of the egg. So, when using this method (which I feel is best for beginners in spite of this problem), remember to put the two halves together often, adjusting the position of any trims that might cause problems later.

THE HINGE SITE:

At this point you have a marked goose egg, you know which hinge you are going to use, and you know that you will be cutting the egg all the way around so you can work on the pieces separately.

Next, you need to mark the hinge site on the egg. For the egg to open straight, you must put the hinge at the *FATTEST* part, even though it isn't in the "center" *(Fig. 5).* The natural tendency is to put the hinge at the center of the egg, but the egg would then open at an angle. (You may want to do this deliberately sometime, just to give the egg more interest.) Position the hinge on the egg and mark around it with a pencil. Lightly sand the area where the hinge will be glued so the glue will stick better.

Before cutting the egg, you must decide whether you want the hinge post to be positioned facing the inside or the outside of the egg. (The hinge itself is on the outside of the egg, but the post may be facing in or out *(Fig. 6-A).*) If it is facing out, the egg will open all the way back. If it is facing in, the egg will only open as far as the hinge will let it. Take a look at a hinge and you will see what I mean. If you decide to put the post to the inside, you will need to cut a little slit for it to fit into. Do this before cutting anything else, checking to be sure the hinge post will fit *(Fig. 6-B).*

PREPARING THE HINGE:

Before being attached, the hinge itself needs a little work done on it. First, be sure it is free of dirt or oil of any kind, and sand it a little where the glue will be to help it stick better. Since it is flat, and the egg is curved, it needs to be bent a little to fit. Don't bend the post itself, just the outer edges *(Fig. 7).*

Make sure the hinge works freely. If it doesn't, you may break your egg trying to open and close it. If your hinge is too tight, carefully pry up (just a little!) on one or more of the flanges which hold the pin in place. (I use an old, dull knife for this.) Don't loosen the flanges too much or it might fall apart.

Getting glue in the hinge post can be a disaster! To prevent this, apply vaseline or liquid soap to the post **ONLY** with a tooth pick. Be sure NOT to get it where you want the glue to stick!

CUTTING THE EGG: *(For applying the hinge half at a time)*

Now you are ready to cut the egg in half. Use a power tool and a diamond cutter or one of the emery cutting wheels. Remember to let the tool do the work. You might want to start your cut at the hinge site, so any uneven spots that may result will be hidden under the hinge. (For more information, see the Cutting and the Projects chapters.)

APPLYING THE HINGE: *(Half at a time)*

Support your egg on something that will hold it securely, such as a small towel that can be bunched up to cradle it. Carefully tape the egg together and place the hinge in position on it. The post should be perfectly straight with the cut. Tape one half of the hinge to the egg. (I like paper tape for this, the kind you get in the medical supplies section of drug stores.) *(Fig. 8)*.

Always use epoxy for hinges, and always have everything ready BEFORE you mix it. Squeeze out equal amount of the two parts onto a little piece of cardboard, and mix them thoroughly with a tooth pick. (There are different schools of thought on how long to mix epoxy, but thirty seconds is more than ample for the glue to set up properly. It is alright to mix longer so the glue is more tacky when you use it, but don't wait too long!)

Using a tooth pick, apply a small amount of epoxy to the under-side of the free half of the hinge, being careful to keep it out of the hinge post. You want to use enough glue to make good contact with the egg. but not so much that it will be forced into the post when the hinge is pressed in place against the egg. (Experience will be your best teacher here. Just keep in mind that it is better to use too little than too much). Now, carefully press the hinge against the egg. Do not handle the egg again until the glue has thoroughly set.

When you have decorated both halves of the egg, and are ready to attach the other half of the hinge, put the egg together and secure it with rubber bands. Be sure the alignment is correct. Apply epoxy to the free half of the hinge, as you did before, and gently press it in place against the egg.

VARIATIONS:

To apply a hinge in one step, cut only the hinge site, plus a 1/2" margin on either side. (This margin will prevent you from running into the hinge with your tool when you complete the cut *(Fig. 6-B)*.) Shape the hinge to the egg, and apply glue to both halves at once. Carefully place the hinge in position on the egg. Tape is not used in this method, so you must position the egg so the hinge is straight up while the glue dries *(Fig. 9)*, otherwise it will slide out of position and become attached where it isn't supposed to be! (See the Trouble Shooting chapter for how to handle this and other problems with epoxy.)

It is possible to put a hinge on the inside of an egg, but this severely limits how far the egg can be opened, and causes problems with the trim around the outside edges. It is a difficult procedure to do, especially if you are working with only one opening. A hinge on the inside might be nice because it doesn't show from the outside, but the problems involved far outweigh this one benefit.

MISCELLANEOUS:

What if your egg won't open after hinging? If your egg hasn't previously been open, the problem may not be a stuck hinge. It is possible that the membrane inside the egg is holding it shut. (This is particularly common with goose eggs.) To free it, slip a knife blade through the opening and cut the membrane. If this doesn't work, it probably is the hinge.

Glue doesn't stick to an Ostrich egg very well, so be sure to rough up the hinge site! Coarse sand paper will do, but I like to use a Dremel and a diamond cutting disc to score the hinge site with little criss-crosses. It is easy to do this at the same time the cut for the hinge is made. Glue will really stick in these little grooves! (I also do this on rhea and emu eggs.) In addition to this, once the hinge is glued in place, I like to drill through the hinge holes and epoxy eyelets *(Plate 5 Page 16)* in them, putting more epoxy on from inside the egg. A hinge rarely comes off after this treatment, unless the egg is mishandled in some way, or there is a problem with the epoxy itself.

Since bare hinges are not attractive, you will be covering them with decorative findings, braids or other materials, as the egg is decorated. This has the dual advantage of enhancing the appearance of the egg, and adding that much more strength to the hinge.

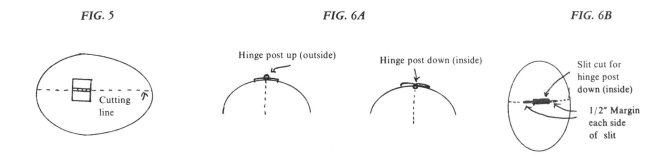

| FIG. 5 | FIG. 6A | FIG. 6B |

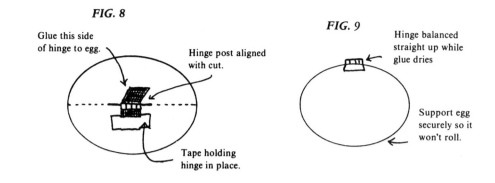

FIG. 7

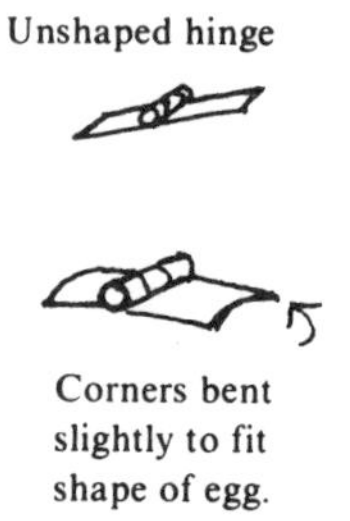

Unshaped hinge

Corners bent
slightly to fit
shape of egg.

FIG. 8

Glue this side
of hinge to egg.

Hinge post aligned
with cut.

Tape holding
hinge in place.

FIG. 9

Hinge balanced
straight up while
glue dries

Support egg
securely so it
won't roll.

CHAPTER X ❧ LINING THE EGG

Lining a jewel box is one of the most important things you will do to it. After all, when you open it what you see inside is the lining, so you want it to look as nice as possible. There are several types of linings, some quite simple, some very elaborate. Two types will be discussed here.

There are a few things to consider, though, before getting started. One is keeping the top of the jewel box from falling back when it is opened. Three ways to do this are: to put the hinge on with the post to the inside (already discussed in the chapter on Hinging); to epoxy findings to the outside of the hinge after the egg is complete (these will touch when the egg is opened, preventing it from falling back); and putting a short length of chain on the inside of the egg as you line it.

Next, you need the right material. Personal preferences will come into play here, but you will want to choose a color and weight of material that will complement the overall theme of the egg.

Last, remember that the egg is an odd shape and cannot be lined like a square jewel box, whose lining is simply glued flat. The curve of the egg makes this type of lining a monumental task, and the results are rarely satisfactory, so it is best to avoid this method.

Following are two tried-and-true methods for lining which are both easy and attractive. Both sets of instructions call for goose eggs, cut in half horizontally, but can be easily adapted to other sized eggs and other cuts.

METHOD ONE: The Puffy Lining. (This lining lays in loose folds in the egg.)

Materials Needed:
1. The egg. (Separate pieces are easiest to work with.)
2. Lining material. (Lets use velvet. A 12 x 12″ piece should be ample for eggs up to a goose egg.)
3. A needle and thread. (Thread should match the material.)
4. Tacky glue.
5. Two pairs of scissors, one large for cutting the fabric, and one small for working inside the egg.
6. Six inches of fine chain.
7. Pencil.
8. Contrasting thread or chalk.
9. Epoxy glue.

TECHNIQUE:

1. Preparing the egg:
Scrape the membrane around the edges of both halves of the egg, to a distance of 1/2″ back from the cut edge. The lining and cording will be glued to this scraped area, giving it better contact with the egg. Use any sharp instrument, such as the point of your manicure scissors *(Fig. 10)*.

2. Cording:
Finishing the inside of your jewel box with cording, made of the same fabric as the lining, will give it the perfect touch. (Braids may be used instead, but they don't have the same elegance.)

To make the cording, cut two bias strips, each 5/8″ wide, from the center of the velvet (cut corner to corner) *(Fig. 11)*. Spread glue over the entire back of each strip, being sure it is well covered, especially along the center. (If it isn't, the cording will come apart later when trimmed.) Gently fold each in half lengthwise, making two long, narrow strips *(Fig. 12)*.
(NOTE: Be sure to use enough glue to make good contact, but not so much that it will soak through the fabric. Be neat! Don't get glue on the nap of the velvet, and don't mash the nap. It is important to have a very light touch when working with fabric and glue!) When the strips have dried, trim them close to the folded edge, making two long, thin lengths of cording *(Fig. 12)*. (If you are using a thinner material, try putting string in the center of the cording to give it body.)

3. The Lining:
The two triangular-shaped pieces of velvet will be the top and bottom linings. Centering half of the egg, cut-side down, on the back of one of the pieces of velvet, lightly pencil an oval, making it about 1 1/2″ larger around than the egg. Do the same on the other piece. (The size of the oval can be adjusted as desired, keeping in mind that the larger the oval is, the more "puffy" the lining will be. It is better to start with a large oval, and be able to cut it down if necessary, than to start with one too small and be stuck with it!) *(Fig. 13)*.

When you have marked the ovals, cut them out and mark each quarter, using chalk or thread of a contrasting color.

These will be reference marks used for properly placing the lining in the egg. Once this is done, baste around the edges of each oval, using matching thread, and gather *(Fig. 14)*.

4. The Chain:

If you are going to be putting a chain in your egg, you may glue one end in place before putting in the lining. Do the top of the egg first, picturing the inside as though it were a clock, with the hinge at the six o'clock position. Epoxy one end of the chain at the ten o'clock position, leaving 1/4" of space at the edge of the egg for cording to fit into later *(Fig. 15)*.(Using epoxy for this will speed things up so you can move right on to the next step). Remember to scrape the membrane where you will be putting the glue.

5. Installing Lining:

When the chain is securely in place, position the velvet in the egg, nap-side up. Match the reference marks on the velvet with the quarters of the egg. Begin gluing the edge of the lining in place around the egg, leaving a space about 3/16" wide for the cording to fit into later. Work all the way around, covering the end of the chain, and spacing the gathers evenly. The reference marks will help with this. (Remove the reference marks once the lining is in place.)

6. Installing Cording:

Glue cording in place at the edge of the velvet, starting at the center front. (Starting here will hide the joint in the cording from view.) The cut edge of the cording should be against the edge of the velvet, so only the folded edge shows. Do not glue the chain under the cording. It should come out between the cording and the lining. Check periodically to be sure the cording doesn't extend over the edge of the shell where it could interfere with the closing of the egg. Make a neat joint where the ends of the cording meet.

7. Putting the Chain in the Bottom:

Select a spot for the other end of the chain that will allow it to fall neatly inside when the egg is closed. The eight o'clock position should be about right, but you may want to try it in a few positions as you open and close the egg before making a final decision Once you have marked the spot for the chain, glue the lining in place as you did the top, but leave this spot open for inserting the chain later.

8. Finishing:

If the egg is in two sections, epoxy the hinge in place. Using tacky, glue the free end of the chain under the lining, checking to be sure that the length of the chain will allow the egg to stand open but not fall too far back *(Fig. 16)*. Allow plenty of drying time. If you try to rush this process, you could pull the chain out and have to do it over!

When the chain is thoroughly dry, glue the cording in place as you did for the top half, starting in the center front. Close the egg often as you work to be sure the two halves join properly. Adjust any cording that might be holding them apart.

METHOD TWO: The Padded Lining. This lining is neater in appearance than the puffy lining, but takes more time and work.

Materials Needed:

1. The Egg.
2. Lining material. (For a goose egg, you will need a piece about 7" wide by 18" long, and four smaller strips, 5/8" wide by 12" long, all cut on the bias).
3. Needle and matching thread.
4. Six inches of fine chain. (Optional).
5. Chalk or thread of another color.
6. Two pairs of scissors, one large and one manicure.
7. Tacky glue.
8. Pencil
9. Epoxy glue
10. Cardboard (such as matte board for picture framing) 3 x 6".
11. Cotton or Fiber-Fill. (Very small amount.)

TECHNIQUE:

1. Prepare the Egg:

Scrape the membrane as for the puffy lining.

2. Cording:

This is the same as for the puffy lining, except you will need four strips.

3. Lining:

If you are putting a chain in, install one end now. Cut two strips of fabric, each 1 1/2" wide by about 18" long. The length and width can be adjusted to give the amount of gathering and fullness desired. Using chalk or contrasting thread, mark four even divisions on one edge of each strip. These reference marks will help you center the strip in the egg evenly. Baste close to both edges of each piece, having the loose ends of thread at the same end of the strip. (This is so the gathers may be easily adjusted as needed during gluing *(Fig. 17)*.

Gather a strip and try it in the egg. If it is too full, cut it to the size desired. Begin gluing it in place, starting at the center front. Turn the end under as you start, so the cut edge doesn't show.

Continue gluing all the way around until the edges meet. Turn the end under as you glue it so it blends with the gathers. The bottom edge of the velvet may be spot-glued in place. It doesn't need to be glued as thoroughly as the top. (Neatness isn't a problem here either, since it will be under the padded "floor"), but it should be held firmly in place. Scrape the membrane where the glue will go.

Repeat this for the other half of the egg, leaving an open spot for the chain, if you are using one.

4. The Padded "Floors".

Cut two ovals of cardboard. (The size will depend on how high you want the floor to be in the egg. You be the judge of this.) When the ovals are cut, glue a little cotton or Fiber-Fill to one side. Very little will do! You only want enough to give a little lift to the velvet.

Cut two ovals of velvet about 3/4" larger around than the cardboard ovals. Cut darts around the edges so when the velvet is glued in place it won't have large, over-lapping areas. Be sure not to make the darts so deep that they will show on the front! When this is done, position them over the padding and glue the tabs to the back of each oval *(Fig. 18)*. As always, be neat with the glue!

When the "floors" are dry, glue them in place in the two

halves of the egg. Use plenty of glue, but don't let it show! Press the floors firmly in place against the gathers.

Neatly edge each floor with cording.

5. Installing The Cording.

Do this the same as for the puffy lining, being sure not to glue the chain under it, and checking often to see that the egg closes properly.

FIG. 10

1/2" membrane scratched

FIG. 11

2 - 5/8" bias strips of fabric.

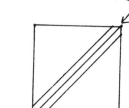

FIG. 12

Cording

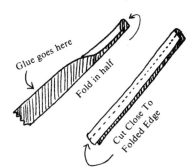

Glue goes here

Fold in half

Cut Close To Folded Edge

FIG. 13

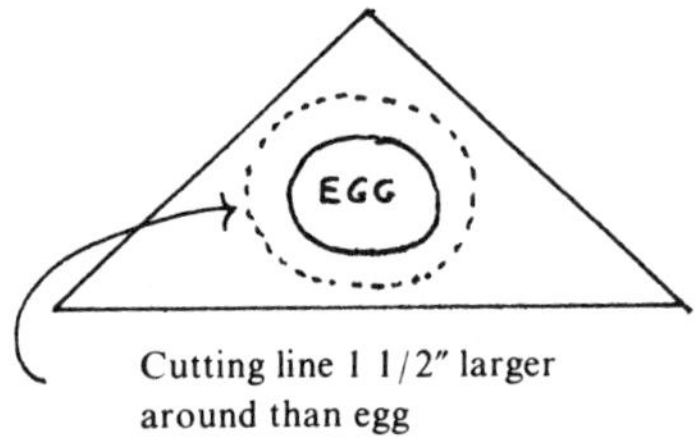

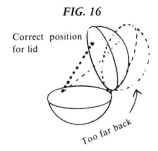

EGG

Cutting line 1 1/2" larger around than egg

FIG. 14

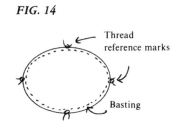

Thread reference marks

Basting

FIG. 15

Inside top of egg

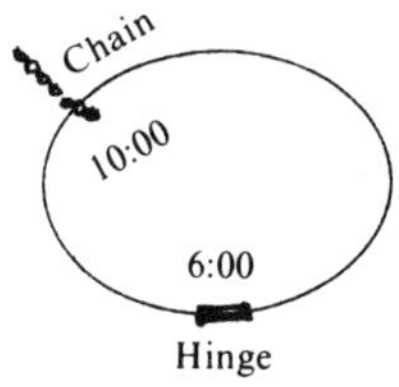

Chain

10:00

6:00

Hinge

FIG. 16

Correct position for lid

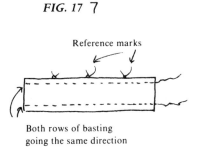

Too far back

FIG. 17

Reference marks

Both rows of basting going the same direction

FIG. 18

Fabric

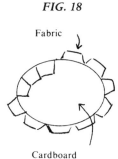

Cardboard

CHAPTER XI   MISCELLANEOUS TIPS & HOW-TO'S

1. USING BROKEN EGGS:

The main thing here is not to discard a salvageable egg. The trouble-shooting chapter will explain how to mend the egg, but you will have to figure out what you want to do with it from there!

There are several ways to treat a mended egg so the breaks won't show. One is to cut away part, or all, of the broken area, blending the cut into the theme of the egg. Another way is to cover the cracks using any one of a variety of decorating methods, including decoupage, beading, or any of the sprinkle-on finishes. Modeling paste is also useful for concealing cracks and other blemishes!

If an egg is just not repairable, use it for practice, or experimenting, or use the pieces for making a mosaic design on another egg!

2. STRENGTHENING EGGSHELLS:

Almost anything done to an egg during the decorating process will add strength to it. Each layer of paint or finish, and everything that is glued to the shell, inside or out, plays its part. But there are some eggs which will need a little extra strengthening to withstand the cutting and handling they will be subject to. These will include the very tiny eggs and, at times, larger but thinner-shelled eggs.

It is an easy matter to strengthen the shells. Simply coat them several times with any finish you choose. Four or five coats should be ample for most eggs. (You might find it harder to cut an egg that has been coated, because the coating sometimes gums up the cutting blade. It may also leave rough edges on the egg itself where the finish has been heated to the melting point by the blade. These will need to be lightly sanded.)

3. FRAYED BRAID:

Have you ever cut a piece of braid, only to have the ends unravel before you can get it on the egg? This can be a real nuisance, especially when you are cutting lots of little pieces. The solution is simple. Just coat the braid with any water-base finish, or even Elmer's Glue. The easiest way is to get some on your fingers, and run the braid or cord through them, coating the full length of it. When it is dry, you can cut it anywhere without having to worry about raveling or fraying.

It is also a good idea to coat braid already on an egg to prevent fraying, especially if it is going to be handled much. If you are putting a finish on your egg, just coat the braid, too.

4. THOSE AWFUL GAPS!

One common problem with jewel boxes and other hinged eggs are gaps that show when the egg is closed. This may be caused by uneven cutting or from trims that hold the two pieces apart. If nothing can be done to correct the problem itself, the next best thing is to cover it up. It is usually a good idea to decorate the inside of a hinged egg before doing the outside-for this very reason, because the trims put on the outside can usually be made to camouflage these unsightly gaps.

When putting the trim on the outside, do one edge first, putting the trim right at the very edge of the cut. Close the egg, or put it together, checking for neatness as you work.

Once this is glued in place, start on the other edge. This is the crucial part. The trim you put on this edge must meet the trim on the other edge, or the gaps will still show. As you glue the trim on, scoot it against the other trim. It will probably overlap the edge of the egg in places but this is all right. Just be sure the trim you are using is wide enough to do the job!

5. EMPTYING HOLES: WHAT TO DO WITH THEM.

The holes in the ends of the eggs can be a real nuisance! All too often they are ragged or off-centered, or both, and must be camouflaged by some means.

There are several ways to do this. Perhaps the design of the egg itself is such that one hole, or maybe both, will be covered by a finial, stand, or other decoration. If this is the case, great! (Be sure to check the inside of the egg, too, because you don't want holes to show here either!)

The holes that won't be covered in the normal decorating process are another matter. They must be filled so they match the egg as closely as possible. If the egg is to be cut, wait until after the cutting is done so you can work from inside the egg.

To fill a large hole, such as one in an ostrich egg, use the epoxy-and-paper-towel method. Put a piece of tape over the hole on the outside of the egg (assuming you are working with a cut egg). Paper tape will do nicely. Mix epoxy with just a little paper-towel, and dab it in the hole from inside the egg, smoothing it as much as possible. Set the egg, hole-side-down, over a cup or other object that won't touch the tape, and let it dry thoroughly. Remove the tape. The epoxy may be a little sticky where it was in contact with the tape, but this is alright. This method may be used on any egg, but it isn't necessary to use the paper-towel on small holes. (Water putty may be used in place of epoxy, but you will have to allow plenty of drying time!)

For uncut eggs the problem is a little different. One way to fill these holes is to tear off a small piece of paper-towel, barely larger than the hole itself. (Tear it, because cutting leaves hard edges that don't smooth down well.) Cover both sides with tacky glue and place it over the hole, smoothing the edges against the egg. The part over the hole itself will sink in a little no matter what you do, so let it dry this way, and later fill it with a tiny amount of epoxy or water putty. When this has dried, gently sand it smooth and level with the egg.

6. PAINTING AN EGG:

Some eggs will take paint much easier than others. Goose eggs will take any kind of paint easily because of the pourous surface, but a duck egg is another matter. The paint seems to almost slide off at times! But it can be done with a little work.

First you need the right kind of paint. My favorite is Duncan's Nonfiring Bisque Stain, which is water-base, comes in a jar, gives good coverage, has beautiful colors, and is readily available from most ceramic supply stores. (I am sure that other brands of ceramic paints are just as good!) For some reason, acrylic paints, especially those in tubes, just don't do as well. They do not go on as smoothly, and brush-marks always seem to show, so I don't use them.

Next you need the right brush. Use one that is wide and flat with soft bristles. A round brush will always leave brush-marks.

Finally, use the right technique. Don't over-load your brush, and spread the paint as far as it will go. Put on several thin coats and you will have a perfect paint job when you are finished!

TIP:

Never shake jars of paint or finish to mix the contents. Stir them instead, and wipe the edges after use. This will prevent stuck lids.

7. SOFTENING A BRITTLE EGG FOR CUTTING:

Ever notice how nicely a fresh egg from the refrigerator cuts? It is because of the moisture. The shell hasn't dried out and become brittle. Soaking brittle eggs for an hour or two, or even over night, will make them easier to cut.

8. PUTTING EGGS ON STANDS STRAIGHT:

It is very disappointing to complete an egg and later notice that it is not straight on the stand, or that the finial (the decoration on the very top of the egg) is leaning to one side! This won't happen if you will follow a few simple rules.

"Eyeing" is the key to getting everything straight! You can't "eye" from above the egg, but must be at "eye-level" to do the job right. Also, two sets of eyes are better than one.

Materials Needed:
A)   A straight stand. (If the stand is crooked, usually the egg will be, too.)
B)   A level table to work on.
C)   A small turntable. (Optional, but handy.)
D)   Another person to help do the eyeing.
E)   Epoxy and shredded paper-towel. (You should be the judge of how much of each, but a 2 x 2" piece of towel, torn into little bits, should be ample. Mix enough epoxy to saturate the towel.)
F)   The egg.
G)   The finial, if there is to be one. (I like to put this on last so it is straight with the egg and stand.)

Technique:

Have everything ready on the table before you mix the glue! When the epoxy and paper-towel are mixed, glue the egg to the stand, positioning it carefully. You and your helper should be at eye-level to the egg, and seeing the egg at right-angles to each other, not from across the table. As you look at the egg, slowly turn it (this is where the turntable comes in handy!) so it can be seen from all sides. If it looks right to both of you, it is probably as straight as it can get! Remember, the glue is setting up as you do this, so don't waste time!

The same method may be used for the finial.

9. WET-SANDING:

This is using your sandpaper wet instead of dry. Decoupaged eggs are best sanded this way. Simply dip the sandpaper in water every so often as you sand. It takes specially made sandpaper to do this, so be sure you are using the right kind. A tip for making the sandpaper glide more easily over the egg is to add a little liquid dish soap to the water. It is surprising how this helps!

Be sure the finish on the egg is dry before trying to sand it, and don't worry if the egg turns milky during sanding - it will clear up when it dries. Avoid getting water in your egg by holding your fingers over the holes.

10. LIFTING A PRINT:

Lifting a print means to take the colored portion of a print off the paper or cardboard it is mounted on. There are several products which will do this (see the section on Glues & Finishes), and each one will give instructions. However, there are a few things you can do to make it easier. One is to use very warm, even hot, water to soak the prints in. (Don't boil them, though!) Also, use a little liquid dish soap in the water. For some reason this helps. Allow plenty of soaking time. The thicker the paper, the longer it takes.

When you are ready to peel the print off, lay it paper-side down on a flat surface, and begin peeling from one corner. (It

helps to trim the edges before peeling). It is almost impossible to get all the paper off on the first try. The residue can be gently rubbed off while holding the print under warm water.

To store lifted prints, place them between layers of paper-towel or waxed paper. If they touch each other, or get folded back on themselves, and stay that way for any length of time, they will stick together. (If this happens, try soaking them in warm water to separate them.) When you are ready to use them, soak them in warm water for a few seconds to make them soft and pliable again.

11. LIGHTING:

I am not going to go into great detail about this, but will give enough information for you to be able to do a lighted egg if you want to. All you really need to know is what supplies to have, and how to put them together so the light will work when you push the switch. The design for the egg, and putting in the lighting, will be up to you. It isn't hard, and once you have done the projects in the back of the book, you should be ready to give it a try!

Materials Needed:
A)   Miniature 1.5v light bulb with wires (or bulb and socket with wires - with this type the bulbs can be changed.)
B)   A 1.5v battery (a AAA size is good.)
C)   A battery holder (a little metal clip with places to attach the wires.)
D)   A miniature switch (the kind with holes in the prongs to hook the wires to are best. Pressure switches, those that are "on" only while pressure is applied, will prevent prematurely burned out bulbs and batteries.)
E)   Extra wire, about 6", to connect the battery to the switch. (You may need even more if the wires from the light are too short.)
F)   Liquid solder, or solder and soldering iron.

Now that you know what you need, here is a diagram showing you how to connect everything so it will work. The placement of each of these things in your egg and/or stand will be up to you! A light in a simple diorama egg makes an interesting added touch, and it isn't hard to do at all! Give it a try!

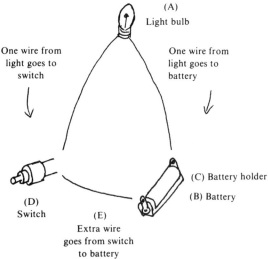

(A) Light bulb

One wire from light goes to switch

One wire from light goes to battery

(C) Battery holder
(B) Battery

(D) Switch
(E) Extra wire goes from switch to battery

NOTE: Be sure to locate the battery where it can be changed easily!

12. DECOUPAGE:

Briefly, decoupage is the art of applying a print, or part of a print, to any surface, and completely burying it in layers of finish until it is perfectly smooth. Doing this on an egg is quite different from doing it on a flat surface, because paper doesn't easily conform to the shape of an egg.

The print itself is cut away from the background, leaving only the main design, which is then applied to the egg using any water-base glue or finish. It may be necessary to cut slits, or even remove small sections of the print, to make it conform to the curved shape of the egg.

Once the print is on as smoothly as you can get it, begin putting coats of whatever finish you choose over it. (If you are using a nonwater-base finish be sure the print is perfectly dry before starting, or you will have moisture problems later.) I usually use Regal Egg Sheen, both to apply the print and as a finish, wet sanding after every five or six coats. You may prefer some other type of finish. Use the product that works best for you, applying enough coats to produce the desired results. Thicker prints will require more coats. The more coats you apply, the more beautiful your egg will be.

Wet sanding every so often will smooth down the edges of the print and get rid of brush marks. A final coat or two of some other product may be put on over the Egg Sheen to give it a bisque look or a high shine. Again, be certain that the egg is thoroughly dry before doing this!

13. RAISED DECOUPAGE (also known as Bas Relief and Paper Tole)

This is different from regular decoupage in that after the background is cut away, each individual component of the print is cut apart, shaped, and glued onto the egg, recreating the original pattern or making an entirely new one. The overall effect is lovely, and once you have tried it, you will not want to go back to plain decoupage! It isn't hard to do, either!

Materials Needed:
1. A suitable print (one that has a definate pattern and is the right size for the egg you are working on).
2. The egg.
3. Regal Egg Sheen. (Or any water-base finish.)
4. Decoupage scissors. (Manicure scissors are fine.)
5. Wooden flower tools or French modeler, (see tools).
6. Tacky Glue.
7. Paper towels.
8. Tweezers.
9. Ceramic pastelling chalks. (optional).
10. Q—tip or small, stiff-bristled brush. (Optional.)

Technique::

A. Coat the print once with the water-base finish. This gives it a little extra body for the shaping process. When this has dried, carefully cut out the entire design, cutting away all the background. Do not cut the print into individual pieces all at once! The shaped pieces bear little resemblance to the original flat pieces, so figuring out how they go back together again isn't an easy task!

You can use two prints, decoupaging the first one flat on the egg and, using it as a guide, raise the second one over it. It is easier to get the pieces back in their original positions this way, but the overall appearance is not as delicate and crisp as the raised decoupage alone. Also, doing only the raised decoupage gives you the advantage of being able to rearrange the print.

B. Plan where you want the design to go on the egg, and begin by cutting out one central piece from the print. (Every leaf, petal, branch, or any definable part of the print, is treated as a separate piece). The reason for starting at the middle of the design is that the pieces are smaller after shaping, and starting at the middle ensures that the print will be uniformly smaller all the way around, and not off-centered.

C. After cutting the first piece, place it face down on any soft, spongy surface, such as several layers of paper towel. Using one of the tools, shape the paper by pressing on the back. Cup the edges. When this has been done, pick it up with tweezers and apply tacky glue, putting glue only on the spot, or spots, that will actually be in contact with the egg. (If you put glue over the entire back, the piece will loose its shape.) Position the piece on the egg. Repeat this process until the entire print is on the egg. (You will easily learn how to shape different kinds of things, from flowers and leaves to people and animals. And you will love the results!)

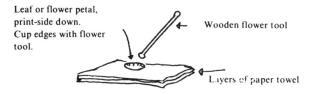

Leaf or flower petal, print-side down. Cup edges with flower tool.

Wooden flower tool

Layers of paper towel

D. When the print is on the egg, put one coat of Egg Sheen over the entire project, egg and all. Now is when I like to use the ceramic pastelling chalks! Using a Q-tip or small, stiff-bristled brush, apply a little color around the print, in effect replacing some of the background that was cut away. You can even alter some of the colors in the print itself, but don't over do it! Too much will detract from the egg!

E. Give the entire project one more coat of Egg Sheen, and then begin putting coats just on the raised portion. This will harden the raised areas, making them durable enough for handling. The number of coats will depend on how "raised" the paper is. Use eight to ten heavy coats on the parts that stand up the most, less on the lower spots. Be neat as you work, keeping the finish only on the raised areas and not getting it on the egg. Little drips will show because they cannot be wet-sanded! When a sufficient number of coats have been applied, let the egg dry thoroughly. Then coat with Deep Flex Bisque Glaze or Glostique, if desired.

CHAPTER XII ✍ TROUBLE SHOOTING

Remember Murphy's Law, mentioned in the chapter on Points To Consider? Well, this is the chapter which, hopefully, will help you get out of some of the difficult spots you might find yourself in.

Here are some of the more common problems, and what you can do to correct them.

1. BROKEN EGG (not as common as you might think!)

If the egg is in few enough pieces, it can be glued back together. Use epoxy for this, having all the pieces ready to assemble before mixing it. Glue only a piece or two at at time, giving each time to set up before adding more pieces. A little tape will help hold it together.

If you need more strength, and don't care too much about looks, you can put a patch in, or on, the egg. Use one layer of paper towel torn (not cut) into strips. (Tearing leaves soft edges that can easily be smoothed down against the egg.) Smear Elmer's glue on both sides and apply it to the break. This technique is helpful on small eggs where the shell is thin. Again, tape will help keep it in shape while the glue is drying.

No matter how good a job you do, mended places will always show. Information on how to hide them is in the Miscellaneous Tips & How-To's chapter.

2. PROBLEMS WITH EPOXY:

(A) *It won't harden.* Are you mixing it right? Be sure to follow the directions on the label. You should be using equal parts of the resin and hardener, and mixing long enough to do a thorough job (thirty seconds is plenty of time). If this doesn't cure it, the problem may be high humidity. Try using a little more hardener. This should do the trick.

(B) *How to unglue it.* At one time it was a disaster if you had an egg that was crooked on its stand, a hinge that wouldn't open, a music-box that quit playing, etc., and they were glued with epoxy, because anything that was glued with epoxy was glued forever, or so we thought. But someone (bless them!!) discovered that epoxy can be unglued by applying heat. Several methods, including hot water, soldering irons, and hair dryers, will all work, but I like the hair dryer method best. Water has obvious drawbacks, and soldering irons only put heat in one small spot at a time, and sometimes scorch it, too, so the hair dryer is best. And nearly everybody has one.

To use it, just aim and blow! Be prepared to spend some time at it, especially if there is a lot of glue, or a large area, involved.

3. PROBLEMS WITH FINISHES:

A) *Paints changing color or bleeding.* This was touched on in the chapter on Glues and Finishes. Some products will react with each other, ususlly unfavorably. Water-base paints will often change color or "bleed" if finishes, such as Deep Flex Bisque Glaze or Glostique, are used over them. Once this has happened, all you can do is paint it over again, this time using a sealer between the paint and the finish. It is a hard lesson to learn, and much easier to prevent than to correct! Always try the products you wish to use on a practice piece first. Then you will know whether to use them on your egg or not.

B) *Globbed (for lack of a better word) water-base finishes.* Strangely enough, some water-base finishes will occasionally coagulate into little globs when put on over paint, or they may cause the paint to come off the egg in spots. This has happened using Egg Sheen over both ceramic paints and acrylic paints, but it doesn't happen every time! It is just some unexplainable phenomenon that occasionally plays havoc with a finish! Again, a sealer over the paint will help.

Avoid over-brushing any finish. If you keep brushing in one spot, trying to smooth the finish, globbing will occur because you are disturbing the part of the finish which has already begun to dry.

If this globbing occurs, don't try to do anything with it while it is still wet. Set the egg aside to dry thoroughly. then lightly sand the affected area and begin again.

C) *Cracked finish.* This is usually caused by putting a nonwater-base finish, such as Glostique, over a water-base finish that hasn't dried thoroughly. Trapped moisture will cause cracking or clouding, and may show up days, or sometimes weeks, after the egg is done. The problem itself cannot be corrected, but you can at times camouflage it by covering it with another type of finish.

D) *Paint Won't Stick.* This may happen if the egg has an oily residue on it. (Beware of seemingly innocent things like nail-polish remover! It has oil in it, and cleaning your egg with it can cause problems.) If you suspect this type of problem, thoroughly wash the egg with an abrasive cleaner, and paint it again.

Sometimes the problem is the egg itself. Ostrich eggs are slick, and paint doesn't stick well to them. A few things that will help are: lightly sanding the egg; applying a coat of Gesso before painting; and putting a sealer on over the paint.

4. TARNISHING.

Everyone has had this problem at one time or another. It can usually be avoided by spraying stands and other items with a fixative as soon as you get them, but occasionally you will run into one that tarishes anyway. Soaking in a solution of water, salt and lemon juice will turn the tarnish color to a light silver, which is better, but not perfect, especially if the stand is supposed to be gold!

The easiest way to handle a tarnished stand is to antique it. Use any of the antiquing stains, or even Kiwi's black Scuff Magic shoe polish. The tarnish will never be noticed!

If your egg is painted, try painting the stand to match it. I do this at times even if it isn't tarnished, because I like the look of a matching stand. Or, if you are really ambitious, you could gold leaf it. Nothing is more lovely!

Findings can be treated the same as stands, and for the most part, so can metallic braid.

5. GLUE ON FABRIC.

When I say "glue on fabric" I am not talking about glue that has soaked through from underneath, because too much was used, or glue that has been spilled on it. Nothing will help these problems, short of replacing the fabric.

What I am talking about is the little bit of glue that got there by being on a finger or tool that lightly touched the fabric. If this happens, do something about it right away! If it is epoxy or cement, try using some of the moist towelettes (used for babies) to clean it up, being careful not to rub the glue into the material.

For cleaning up white glue, use moist (not wet) Q-tips, using light, quick strokes. Don't rub! Then lightly brush the nap up with a tooth brush, giving it a second brushing when the area has dried. If the glue still shows, try to cover it with decorations that look like they were supposed to be there in the first place!

6.   THE IMPOSSIBLE EGG:

Sometime in your egging, you will start an egg that never seems to get off the ground. Nothing goes right with it, and you don't like it, but, for some reason, you keep fooling with it, trying this, changing that, rearranging something else. Frustrated, you set it aside for weeks at a time, trying to ignore it, but you keep coming back to it, thinking there must be **SOMETHING** you can do with it. So, you fool with it some more, with the same exasperating results.

When this happens, just give up on it! You will probably never finish it, and if you did, you wouldn't be happy with it, so don't waste your time. Either give it to someone to practice on, or remove anything salvageable from it and pitch it. You are supposed to ENJOY doing eggs, remember?

CHAPTER XIII ❧ PROJECTS

GENERAL INFORMATION:

This section contains complete instructions for doing eight different egg projects. The projects start with an easy egg, offering three ideas for its use. The other five projects become progressively more challenging, each having something new for you to learn. By the time you have finished all eight, you will be ready to move on to the more advanced eggs.

Besides the basics described earlier in the book, you will learn to bead an egg, do both regular and raised decoupage, install a music box, use several of the finishes mentioned in Chapter Five, and much more.

Though all of the eggs in these projects will be cut, many of the techniques you will be learning can easily be applied to uncut eggs. A simple decoupaged egg on a stand or hanging on a Christmas tree is lovely, and I am sure you will enjoy making many of these!

At the beginning of each project there will be a complete list of all the items used. You may adhere to this list exactly, or substitute in any way you like, or find necessary. If the project calls for a duck egg and all you have is a chicken egg, use it! Remember, these projects are just examples for you to learn from and do not have to be copied exactly.

If you have learned a technique different from what is taught here, and you are happy with the results you get, by all means stick with it. As mentioned earlier, there is no single way to do any of this. Try different techniques and select the one that works best for you.

The eggs shown on the covers of the book are different views of the eggs you will be doing in the projects. It will help you to look at the pictures occasionally as you work.

Your original eggs are works of art and should be signed and dated. This is especially important if you are planning to sell them. Prospective buyers will often ask, or look to see, if the egg(s) they are interested in are signed and dated, and may turn them down if they aren't. It is also a good idea to keep a pictorial record of the eggs you make. Photos can be very helpful if you want to duplicate an egg you have sold, or show others what you have done!

Pricing Eggs:

When selling eggs, you will need to know how to price them. This will be determined by several factors, such as the cost of the materials used, the amount of time involved, and the quality of workmanship (a poorly decorated egg will not bring as much as one done carefully and neatly!). Even your geographical location will play a part in what you can charge. You will have to be the judge of all these things, arriving at a price that will compensate you adequately (hopefully) and be satisfactory to your customers as well.

The directions for the following projects assume you are using eggs that have been emptied by being blown out, and so have holes in each end.

Now for the projects!

THE DIORAMA EGGS

A "diorama" egg is generally considered to be an egg with one or more openings and containing a scene. There are no doors or hinges. A "scene" in the case of an egger, may consist of a single figure or object. The egg may hang or be on a stand.

Following are three versions of the diorama egg.

PROJECT ONE:—SINGLE OPENING EGG ON A STAND

1.)   *Supplies used:* (remember, you can substitute!):
      Double-yolk turkey egg.
      Gold metal stand
      Finding for finial (a finial is the decoration on the very top of egg *(Fig. 1).*

Bead for finial - 12mm or so.
One foot of satin cord, pale blue.
Two feet of strung or molded pearls, blue or white.
Light blue paint.
2″ x 2″ piece of cardboard (not thick).
2″ x 2″ piece of light blue velvet or other fabric.
Figure for inside the egg.
Tacky and Epoxy glues.
Manicure scissors.
Large scissors.
Egg Sheen. (Regal Egg Sheen).

2) *Marking and cutting:* (also refer to Chapters VI & VII):

A.   Draw an oval on the egg, being sure the size and shape of the oval suits the egg. Don't make the lower edge of the oval too low because there won't be room inside the egg for the floor if you do (Fig. 2).

B.   Coat the cutting line with Egg Sheen or nail polish only if the egg is to be cut with manicure scissors. (It will gum up the cutting disc of an electric tool.)

C.   Cut out the opening. (Follow the directions in Chapter VI, Method Two. Your egg may already be empty, but most of the directions will be the same.)

3)   Paint the inside of the egg two or three times with the light blue paint. No streaks or brush-marks should show.

4)   Coat the outside three or four times with Egg Sheen. (If you are not using a turkey egg, you may want to paint the outside as well as the inside. You don't have to put anything over the paint if you don't want to, but the outside will eventually get fingerprints and dirt on it, so it is best to put a sealer over the paint, followed by a matte or gloss finish. (See Chapter V)).

5)   Cut a circle of cardboard to use as the floor inside the egg. Cut it so it fits below the level of the opening.

6.) Cover one side of the cardboard with velvet, using Tacky glue. When the velvet has dried, glue the floor into the egg, being sure it is level.

7)   Glue satin cord around the edge of the floor. This will hide the joint between floor and egg. Begin and end at the center back. The figure inside the egg will conceal the joint in the cord.

8)   Glue the figure in place on the floor. You may use epoxy for this if you like. Its fast set-up time will allow you to continue working in a few minutes. If you are using Tacky, plan to do this step last, or at a time when you can leave the project for several hours while the glue dries.

9)   Glue Satin cord around the outside opening of the egg, starting at the center bottom, and gluing it about 1/16th of an inch back from the cut edge.

10) Glue a row of pearls on each side of the satin cord.

11) Epoxy the egg on the base, eyeing it carefully to be sure it is straight. Use the epoxy-paper-towel mixture (See Chapter V & Chapter XI, #5).

12) Glue the metal finding to the center top of the egg. (If there is an emptying hole in the top of your egg, don't use it to center the finding by! It is probably not dead center, and will cause you to have a lop-sided finial!) Glue a bead or large pearl to the finding, completing the finial. You may use Tacky or Epoxy for this.

13) Sign and date your egg.

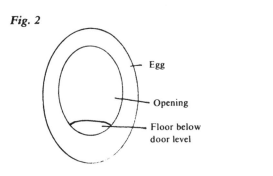

Fig. 1 (actual size)

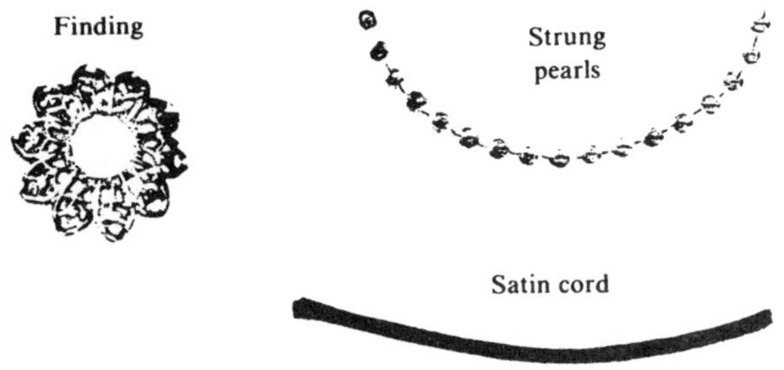

Finding   Strung pearls

Satin cord

Fig. 2

Egg

Opening

Floor below door level

PROJECT TWO: — DOUBLE OPENING HANGING EGG

These are easy to do and are a lot of fun! Make them as Christmas ornaments, for a unique gift, or a bazaar item. This egg has a sprinkle-on finish, which is a good way to hide blemishes and add sparkle at the same time.

1. *Supplies used:*
Duck egg.
Christmas-green paint, water-base.
2 Bead caps (Fig. 3).
2 Head pins (Fig. 3).
4 Beads, two each of two sizes, green. (approx. 6 & 10 mm).
1 1/2 feet of decorative braid *(Fig. 3)*.
Diamond dust.
Cotton ball or Fiber-Fill.
Small wooden house and sisal tree.
2″ x 2″ cardboard.
Spray fixative (spray starch will do).
Tacky glue.
Manicure scissors.

2. *Marking and cutting:* (See Chapters VI & VII):

A.   Draw two ovals on opposite sides of the egg. You will have to eye this by looking at the egg from the ends and sides to see if the ovals are even (Fig. 4). If you are using an electric tool to cut with, mark and cut only one side, then use the cut out piece to mark around for the other side of the egg. If you have an egg marker, you may use this to mark the ovals. Use the adapters if your marker has them, and put the egg in place. With the egg in a horizontal position and the pencil centered, make a small mark on each side of the egg next to the marker *(Fig. 5)*.

Next, rotate the egg in the marker so one of the marks is straight up. Adjust the pencil higher and mark an oval by moving the pencil around the egg *(Fig. 6)*. It might take a few tries to make the oval the size you want, but you will soon learn to judge the position of the pencil correctly. After the first oval has been drawn, rotate the egg so the other mark is straight up. Mark the second oval. Be sure to work on a flat, level surface. (Refer to the directions that came with your marker for additional information).

B.   Coat the lines with Egg Sheen or Nail Polish (cutting with scissors).

C.   Cut out the openings. (Chapter VI, Method Two).

D.   Paint the outside of the egg green, applying enough coats for a smooth finish. (A skewer-type egg holder is helpful here!) Leave the inside of the egg white.

E.   Cut a circle of cardboard to fit inside the egg below the level of the openings. Paint one side white. When this has dried, glue it in the egg painted side up.

F.   Coat the inside of the egg (not the floor) with white glue and pour in a spoonful of diamond dust. Rotate the egg so the diamond dust covers the entire inside.

G.   Sign and date the outside of the egg in a spot that won't be covered with braid or findings. Coat the outside with white glue or Egg Sheen and cover with diamond dust.

H.   Apply a thick coat of Tacky Glue to the floor of the egg, and put a thin layer of cotton or Fiber-Fill over it to simulate snow. While the glue is still wet, apply a generous amount of glue to the bottoms of the house and tree and position them in the egg. This glue should soak through the cotton to the glue beneath, making sure the house and tree are held permanently in place.

I.   Spray the house, tree, and cotton with a fixative, and quickly sprinkle with diamond dust, giving them a sparkly snow effect. This completes the inside.

J.   Glue a row of decorative braid around each opening.

K.   Shape the bead caps, fitting one to the top and one to the bottom of the egg. Pass a head pin through the center hole of each bead cap so the head of the pin is inside the cap *(Fig. 7)*. (If the head of the pin slips through the hole, put a sequin or small bead cap with a smaller hole on the pin first). When the pin is through the bead cap, put one of the larger beads on it, followed by a smaller one. The end of the pin should then be cut about 3/8″ above the smaller bead, and this part bent in a circle with round-nose pliers (rosary pliers) (Fig. 8). This circle will hold the beads in place and form a loop to hook an ornament hanger to.

L.   Apply Tacky to the under-side of one of the bead caps and glue it to one end of the egg. There should be enough glue to soak through the diamond dust and make good contact with the egg. Prop the egg so the bead cap is straight up while the glue dries. When it is thoroughly dry, do the other end.

Fig. 3

(Actual Size)

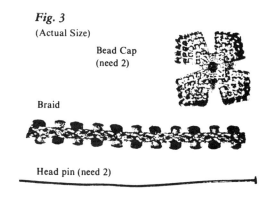

Bead Cap
(need 2)

Braid

Head pin (need 2)

Fig. 4

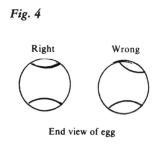

Right   Wrong

End view of egg

Fig. 5

Make a small mark on each side of egg next to platic egg egg marker.

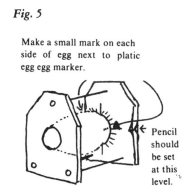

← Pencil should be set at this level.

Fig. 6

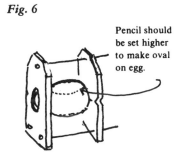

Pencil should be set higher to make oval on egg.

Fig. 7

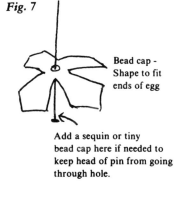

Bead cap - Shape to fit ends of egg

Add a sequin or tiny bead cap here if needed to keep head of pin from going through hole.

Fig. 8

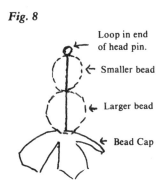

Loop in end of head pin.

← Smaller bead

← Larger bead

← Bead Cap

PROJECT THREE: TRIPLE OPENING HANGING EGG

This egg is a more elaborate version of the Double Opening egg. It takes more time and materials, but the effort is worth it!

1. **Supplies used:**
   Duck egg.
   6" x 6" piece of red velvet.
   1 yard red satin cord **(Fig. 9)**.
   1 yard thin gold cord **(Fig. 9)**.
   2 gold findings "A" **(Fig. 9)**.
   1 head pin **(Fig. 9)**.
   2 12mm beads, red.
   1 gold metal tassel (red satin tassel will do.) **(Fig. 9)**.
   6 size 20ss rhinestones, red **(Fig. 9)**.
   3 findings "B" for sides of egg **(Fig. 9)**.
   3 size 5ss rhinestones, red **(Fig. 9)**.
   Diamond dust.
   6" fine gold chain.
   1 mini-cluster of pinecones and berries.
   Small plastic evergreen foliage.
   Cotton ball or Fiber-Fill.
   Egg Sheen (Regal Egg Sheen).
   Tacky and Epoxy glue.

2. **Marking and cutting:**
   A.   Mark as in the Double-opening egg, making three ovals instead of two. (If you are using the egg marker shown in Chapter V, notice that the plastic ends of the marker are six-sided. For the sake of simplicity, lets number three of the sides *(Fig. 10)*. When the marker is in the normal horizontal position, side-1 is down. When the marker is in this position, the egg in place, and the pencil centered according to the directions that came with the marker, make a small mark on one side of the egg next to the plastic (Fig. 5). To make the next mark, roll the marker so that side-2 is on the table (Fig. 11). (NOTE: ONLY THE EGG MARKER HAS BEEN MOVED! The pencil holder is in the same place and the position of the egg in the marker is the same.) When the second mark has been made, roll the marker to side-3 and make the third mark. You should now have three small marks on your egg, dividing it into even thirds. (The marks should be next to the plastic because it is easier to reposition the egg in the marker with them here than with them somewhere in the center of the egg.) Next, put the marker back to side-1, and rotate the egg so one of the marks is straight up. Raise the level of the pencil to the desired height and mark and oval. Repeat for the other two ovals. Leave a space of about 1/2" between each oval (Fig. 12).

   B.   If you are cutting with scissors, coat the ovals with Egg Sheen.

C.   Cut out the ovals (Chapter VI, Method Two.)

3.   Sign and date the INSIDE of the egg near the top where it won't be hidden by the objects inside, then coat the inside with white glue and cover with diamond dust.

4.   The velvet is cut on the bias and applied in three sections, shaped as shown in (Fig. 13). Mark the top and bottom of the egg into thirds, using the previous marks as guides (Fig. 14). Apply tacky glue to one section and cover with velvet. Trim the velvet to fit within the pencil lines and cut edges of the egg. Repeat with the other two sections. Handle the velvet carefully, so the nap isn't crushed, and don't use too much glue!

5.   Glue satin cord around each opening, hiding the edges of the egg and the velvet. Begin and end at the center bottom of each opening.

6.   Glue satin cord along the joints of the velvet where the dividing lines were, concealing these joints.

7.   Cut six pieces of satin cord, three 2 1/2" long, and three 2" long. (These lengths may be adjusted according to the size egg you are working with.) Glue the longer pieces in place at the large end of the egg in the position shown in (Fig. 15), starting and ending at the point of the egg. Do the same at the other end of the egg with the smaller pieces.

8.   Using narrow gold braid, outline both sides of all the satin cord, except that in the openings (only one side is outlined here). See photo on back cover.

9. Glue a Size 20ss rhinestone in each loop of satin cord (Fig. 15).

10. Shape the three "B" findings to fit the sides of the egg, and glue them in place between each opening. Glue a rhinestone on each of these findings (Fig. 15).

11. Epoxy a finding "A" at each end of the egg, and epoxy a bead to the TOP of the egg only, positioning it so its hole is up-and-down. When the bead is set in place, put epoxy into the hole and poke both ends of the 6" piece of chain into the glue. This will be the hanger.

12. Pass a head pin through the other bead and cut off all but 3/8". Make a loop using round-nose (rosary) pliers. Epoxy the bead over the finding at the other end of the egg, loop-side out. When this has set, attach a tassel to the loop.

13. Glue a little cotton into the bottom of the egg. Put a generous amount of white glue on the cotton and place the pine-cone spray in the center. Place bits of the green foliage around the pine-cones, arranging them so they fill any gaps, letting some of them extend through the openings of the egg. If desired, spray the greenery with a fixative and quickly sprinkle on diamond dust. (Just be careful not to get any spray on the velvet!)

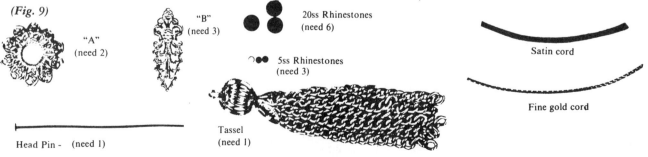

(Fig. 9)

"A" (need 2)

"B" (need 3)

20ss Rhinestones (need 6)

5ss Rhinestones (need 3)

Satin cord

Fine gold cord

Head Pin -   (need 1)

Tassel (need 1)

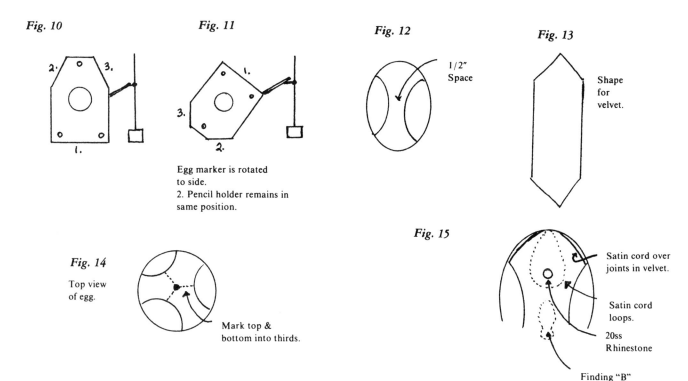

Fig. 10

Fig. 11

Egg marker is rotated
to side.
2. Pencil holder remains in
same position.

Fig. 12

1/2″
Space

Fig. 13

Shape
for
velvet.

Fig. 14

Top view
of egg.

Mark top &
bottom into thirds.

Fig. 15

Satin cord over
joints in velvet.

Satin cord
loops.

20ss
Rhinestone

Finding "B"

PROJECT FOUR: TOOTHPICK HOLDER

This is quick and easy to do, and a handy item to have around the house. Who doesn't use a toothpick holder? (By making a simple change in the cut, you could make a vase instead. Just make a small, round opening at the top of the egg.)

1. *Supplies needed:*
   Chicken egg.
   Suitable stand.
   Small print, enough for both sides (Fig. 16).
   White paint.
   Other paint that will match a color in the print.
   1 foot round, gold cord (Fig. 16).
   1 foot single-loop cord (Fig. 16).
   A flat, 1/2″ paint brush.
   Manicure scissors.
   Sealer (Glosseal).
   Egg Sheen.
   Deep Flex Bisque Glaze (or similiar product).
   Wet/dry sand paper.
   Tacky and Epoxy glues.
   2 small bead caps (Fig. 16).
   Gold paint or pen.

2. *Marking and cutting:*
   A.   Marking this egg is simple. Just draw an elongated oval over the top (the large end, in this case) of your egg (Fig. 17). Eye your oval to be sure it is symmetrical and properly placed on the egg. (If you have an egg marker, it will help you to properly position the oval, but you will still have to draw the oval itself. Put the egg in the marker, and set the marker upright. Make a small mark on each side of the egg approximately two-thirds of the way up (Fig. 18). Lay the marker down, center the pencil, and make a line across the end of the egg between the two marks (Fig. 18). These markings will give you guide-lines to go by when you draw the oval).

   B.   Coat the oval with Egg Sheen (if you are cutting with scissors) and cut it out. If ragged edges occur, trim them with the scissors or smooth them with sand paper or a nail file. Don't lose the shape of the oval.

3.   Paint the inside of the egg with the color that matches your print, putting on enough coats for good coverage.

4.   Paint the outside white.

5.   Coat inside and outside with two coats of sealer.

6.   Carefully cut out the prints you will be using, cutting away all the background. (Manicure or decoupage scissors are best for this.)

7.   Apply the print to the egg (see Chapter XI, #12 Decoupage, and #9 for wet-sanding).

8.   Sign and date the egg.

9.   When the print is "sunk" give it a final wet-sanding and allow it to dry thoroughly. When dry, coat it inside and out with a nonwater-base, matte finish, such as Deep Flex Bisque Glaze or Porcel-It. This will give the egg a rich porcelain look and a protective, water-proof coating.

10. Epoxy small findings (bead caps) over the hole in the bottom of the egg, one inside and one outside. (It isn't necessary to cover the outside hole if it will be hidden by the base.)

11. Paint the cut edge of the egg gold, and glue a row of gold cord on the outside of the edge. Follow this with a row of gold, single-loop braid.

12. Carefully epoxy the egg to its base. (If the base doesn't have a "cup" for the egg to sit in, but is just an oval of metal, don't use paper-towel with the epoxy, or else use very little of it, covering any that shows with braid or other trim (See Chapter XI, Part 2).

13. Finally, put a row of round, gold cord where the egg and stand are joined.

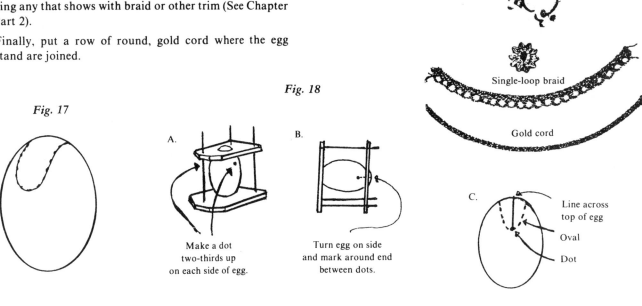

Fig. 16

Single-loop braid

Gold cord

Fig. 18

Fig. 17

A.

Make a dot
two-thirds up
on each side of egg.

B.

Turn egg on side
and mark around end
between dots.

C.

Line across
top of egg

Oval

Dot

PROJECT FIVE: NAPKIN RINGS

In this project, you will again be doing some decoupage, but this time you will "lift" the print. You will also learn to shade with chalks, and apply a crackeled finish. You may use chicken eggs, but duck eggs are better because they are stronger.

The completed napkin rings are useful items, and will prove to be a great conversation piece. And, they make a nice set when matched with the toothpick holder. The directions call for four eggs and will list the supplies needed to complete that number, but you may make as many as you like!

1. *Supplies used:*
   4 duck eggs (matching in size and shape).
   Egg Marker (not an absolute must, but very helpful!)
   4 pieces pale blue velvet, each 2" x 8" long, cut on the bias.
   2 yards round gold cord.
   1 Sonie Ames print #41 (or other print(s) with pieces narrow enough for use in this project.)
   Manicure scissors.
   Ceramic pastelling chalks.
   Ivory paint.
   Sealer (Glosseal).
   Egg Sheen.
   Deep Flex Bisque Glaze.
   Green water-base paint (leaf-color).
   Decal-It & Crackel-It.
   Brown antiquing stain (oil-base).
   1/2" flat brush.
   Wet/dry sandpaper.
   Tacky glue.

2. *Marking and cutting:*
   A. The ends of the eggs will be cut away, leaving only the center portions. These rings of egg should measure 1 1/4" across, and should be taken from the section that will give them the best shape. If cut too far to either end of the egg, they will be wider on one side than the other (Fig. 19).

   B. Using a tape measure or ruler, make two marks on each egg 1 1/4" apart centering at the widest part of the egg. Now hold the egg horizontally at eye-level, with the marks at the top of the egg, and look at the marks (Fig. 20). You should be able to tell by this if they are positioned correctly. Repeat this process with the rest of the eggs, making adjustments in the marks as needed.

   C. If you are using an egg marker, the rest is easy. Just put the eggs in the marker and make lines around them, using the marks as guides. If you aren't using an egg marker, cut a long strip of paper wide enough to fit between the marks (this may be a bit wider than 1 1/4" because of the curvature of the egg). Wrap the paper around the egg as evenly as possible, and use its edges as a guide for your pencil. (A piece of heavy fabric will also work.)

D. If you are cutting with scissors, coat the lines with Egg Sheen. Cut carefully. (See Chapter VIII.)

3. Paint the outsides of the eggs ivory. Leave the insides white.

4. Put two coats of sealer over the paint.

5. Lift only the forget-me-not portion of the print, following the directions on the bottle of Decal-It and the information in Chapter XI, part 10.

6. When the print has been lifted, cut out sections of it and arrange them as desired on the eggs, gluing them in place with tacky, or any other white glue. (You may even use Decal-It.)

7. Coat the entire outside of each egg with two coats of Egg Sheen.

8. Using a tiny, round brush paint little stems here and there around the flowers and leaves. (This step is optional, but it adds a lot to the finished piece.) Sign and date each egg with the same brush and paint.

9. Using the pastelling chalks and a small, stiff-bristled brush or Q-Tip, gently rub a little color around the flowers and leaves. This is easy to over-do, so be careful!

10. Once the chalk is on, carefully apply a coat of Decal-It. Do not rub the brush over the egg since this may cause the chalk to streak.

11. Apply Crackel-It according to the directions on the bottle, and the information in Chapter V, part 5. (NOTE: It is possible

to speed up the curing-time for Crackel-It a little by putting the eggs in a warm, dry place, such as a gas oven with the pilot light on. (Be careful about warming eggs that have epoxy on them, though! Too much warmth, and it might come loose!)

12. When the crackels have formed, rub antiquing stain over the surface, being sure it gets into the "cracks". Then wipe off the excess and let the eggs dry thoroughly.

13. Apply several coats of Egg Sheen (six or eight), and wet-sand until smooth. (See Chapter XI, part 9 for information on wet-sanding.)

14. Add more coats if desired. Then apply two final coats of Deep Flex Bisque Glaze, or a similiar product. This will add beauty and protection to your eggs.

15. To put in the velvet, smear Tacky glue all the way around the inside of one egg. Start behind the decoupaged portion of the egg by placing a strip of velvet in the egg, nap-side up. Begin smoothing it gently against the egg working all the way around (Fig. 21). Remove any excess length by trimming it neatly against the other end of the velvet. If the glue gets a little dry while you are working, add some more. Just be careful not to get it on the nap of the velvet or let it soak through. Repeat this process with the other three eggs.

16. Trim off any excess velvet.

17. Glue round, gold cord to the edges of the eggs using tacky glue. This will hide the cut edges of the eggs and the velvet. Join the cord neatly, adding a little glue at the ends to keep it from raveling.

Fig. 19

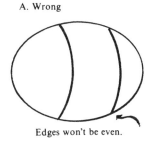

A. Wrong   B. Right

← 1¼" →

Edges won't be even.   Centered at fattest part of egg.

Fig. 20

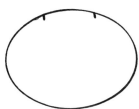

Hold egg so marks are at the top and look at it at eye-level.

Fig. 21

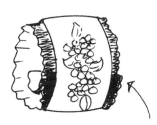

Start velvet behind flowers. Trim all excess.

PROJECT SIX: CRADLE

In this project you will learn to use pearl flakes and do the "puffy" lining. A cradle egg makes a darling gift for a new baby! (Add the baby's name and birthdate somewhere on the egg for a more personal touch). The doll shown in the photographs is 2" long and made of porcelain. (Instructions not included).

If you will be using scissors to cut with, I suggest you soak the egg over night before starting. This will make the egg less brittle.

1. **Supplies used:**
   Goose egg.
   Gold stand for horizontal egg.

Pale pink paint.
Pearl flakes.
12" square of pink velvet.
2 feet delicate white lace, 1/2" wide, ungathered.
1 foot pink satin cord (Fig. 22).
1 foot delicate, single loop gold braid (Fig. 22).
1 foot round, gold cord (Fig. 22).
2 feet pink ribbon, 1/8" wide.
4 size 12ss pink rhinestones.
Tacky & epoxy glues.
1/2" flat brush.
Sealer (Glosseal).

Deep Flex Bisque Glaze.
Egg Sheen.

2. *Marking and cutting:*

A.   Mark a line lengthwise around the egg a little above center. (Use an egg marker if you have one.) On the line you have just drawn, mark two dots, one on each side of the egg, about two-thirds of the way toward the large end (Fig. 23).

B.   Connect the dots by drawing a diagonal line across the top of the egg, slanting it somewhat toward the large end (Dotted line in Fig. 23).

C.   Coat the lines with Egg Sheen and cut carefully with scissors. (An electric tool and diamond cutting disc would be very handy here!) Sand the edges lightly to smooth them. If there are jagged places, just plan to go over them with the trim, as though they weren't there!

3.   To cover the emptying holes, glue a small piece of paper towel over them from inside the egg. On the outside, fill them with water putty (available from a hardware store), plaster-of-paris, or glue. Let dry before painting.

4.   Paint the outside of the egg pale pink and seal the paint with Glosseal, or other sealer.

5.   If your pearl flakes aren't fairly fine in texture, break them up a little. Using a white glue, apply a light sprinkling of the pearl flakes to the entire outside of the egg. Pat them down with your fingers so they don't stand on edge. Do a section at a time.

6.   Coat the pearl flakes five or six times with Egg Sheen, wet-sanding after the last coat. (See Chapter XI, part 9, for information on wet-sanding.)

7.   Apply two final coats of Deep Flex Bisque Glaze.

8.   The lining may be put in now. (See Chapter X, Method One for instructions). Cording will also be used, so follow the directions for that as well.

9.   After the lining and cording are in place (Fig. 24) glue a row of the round, gold cord around the outside of the egg at the very edge. The glue a row of the pink, satin cord over the cut edge of the egg, between the velvet cording and the gold cord. (Looked at from the top, the three cords will be in a row, with the satin cord more elevated).

10.   Loosly gather a 5″ piece of the lace. On the bonnet only, glue the lace into the angle formed by the gold cord and the satin cord (Fig. 24).

11.   Glue gathered lace around the inside of the egg, below the velvet cording (Fig. 24).

12.   Glue ungathered lace against the gold cord around the outside of the egg. On top of this, glue a row of delicate, single-loop gold braid, butting it against the gold cord.

13.   At the bonnet-end of the egg over the glue hole, glue a 3/4″ circle of velvet. Glue a row of satin cord around it (see photo).

14.   Make four "bows" by cutting four 5″ lengths of ribbon. Loop the ribbon into a bow shape, without actually tying a bow. Using a drape stick, or other tool, place a spot of glue between the ribbon where the loops come together. Place the ribbon on some surface (a dry sponge, for instance) and hold it there with a pin (Fig. 25).

15.   When the ribbons have dried, glue one in the center of the circle at the front of the egg, one just below the gold cord at the foot of the egg, and one on each side where the bonnet begins (see photos).

16.   Epoxy the egg to the base, trying to get it in the right spot on the first try. (Adjustments in position after the egg is in the glue could result in glue getting where you don't want it. Minor adjustments should be all right.) Remember to use small amounts of glue—you can always add more around the edges later if needed (see Chapter XI, part 8).

17.   Glue a rhinestone in the center of each ribbon, and tack down the ends of the ribbon with glue to hold them in position.

18.   Glue a row of velvet cording along the edge of the stand where it joins the egg.

19.   Sign and date the egg.

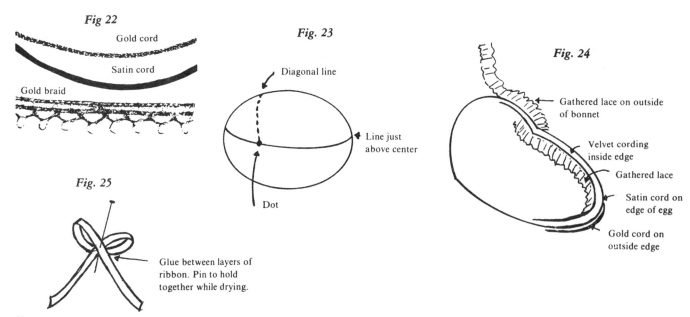

Fig 22
Gold cord
Satin cord
Gold braid

Fig. 23
Diagonal line
Line just above center
Dot

Fig. 24
Gathered lace on outside of bonnet
Velvet cording inside edge
Gathered lace
Satin cord on edge of egg
Gold cord on outside edge

Fig. 25
Glue between layers of ribbon. Pin to hold together while drying.

PROJECT SEVEN: MUSICAL BELL

This egg is challenging, but not difficult. If you have completed the previous projects, you are ready for it. You will learn about raised decoupage, a variation of the "puffy" lining, shading with chalks, and installing a music box. An egg marker and electric cutting tool would be very useful here, but are not vital. If you are cutting with scissors, it will be helpful to soak the egg over night before starting. You *MUST* use a goose egg on this project since a smaller egg would not have room for the music box. Also, the egg should be fairly big around, allowing the music box to fit high enough that the key doesn't stick out the bottom and keep it from sitting level.

1. *Supplies used.*
   Goose egg (approx. 9 1/2 - 10″ around lengthwise).
   Velvet to match print, 12 x 12″. (Beige panne′ was used in model egg shown in the photos.)
   Suitable print (Sonie Ames print #23 Acorns & Leaves).
   Music box (Autumn Leaves).
   Bell handle (lamp finial).
   Bolt and washer (Bolt should fit loosly into bell handle).
   Finding to go under bell handle (Fig. 26).
   Paint (Duncan's Champagne Ice).
   2 feet round, gold cord (Fig. 26).
   1 foot wider braid (optional-may use velvet cording for this (Fig. 26).
   Paint, brown.
   Egg Sheen.
   Sealer.
   Pastelling chalks & small stiff-bristled brush.
   Deep Flex Bisque Glaze.
   1/2″ flat brush.
   Tacky & Epoxy glues.
   Wet/dry sandpaper.
   Needle & thread to match velvet.
   14″ topaz rhinestone chain (Fig. 26).
   Flower tools, or French Modeler.

2. *Marking and cutting:*
   A. Decide which end of the egg you want for the top. (The model egg has the small pointed end as the top). When you have decided, make a small mark on the egg about two-thirds of the way down (Fig. 27). Put a wide rubber band around the egg at this point and try to get it as straight as possible. Eye if from all sides. Then mark a circle around the egg, using it as a guide (dotted line in Fig. 27).

   B. Mark the exact center top of the egg. (If possible, pick an egg with the emptying hole in the center, or nearly so).

   C. Coat the cutting line with Egg Sheen (if cutting with scissors) and carefully cut the egg (see Chapter VIII). Sand the edge smooth.

   D. Make a hole in the center top of the egg, large enough for the bolt to fit through. The hole can be ragged, but should not be much larger around than a pencil.

3. Completely coat the inside of the egg with epoxy to strengthen the shell.

4. Paint the outside of the egg "Champagne Ice". (This paint requires more coats than usual for good coverage (a trait of pearlized paints) so apply whatever number of coats it takes.) Follow this with a coat of sealer and then several coats of Egg Sheen. Wet-sand after six or seven coats. Then put on one more coat.

5. On the outside of the egg, epoxy the finding over the top hole, centering it carefully. When it has dried, epoxy the bell handle to it. Be SURE the bell handle is straight up and down. Look at it from all angles!

6. (Have the bolt and washer ready.) Mix epoxy with a litle paper-towel. Poke some of the mixture into the bell handle from inside the egg, and spread a little around the hole. Quickly place the washer over the hole and put the bolt through it, pressing it into the bell handle as far as it will go. Use the rest of the epoxy around the washer (Fig. 28).

8. Have the music box on hand as you mix another batch of epoxy and paper-towel. Hold the music box by its key and put a generous amount of the epoxy mixture on each corner, on the opposite side from the key. Hold the egg handle-down and place the music box in position, being sure the key is straight up and down within the egg. Let it dry, Mix some more epoxy and paper-towel and pack it between the music box and the egg. DON'T GET GLUE IN OR AROUND THE KEY HOLE!

9. Cut a 5″ circle of velvet and follow the directions for the "puffy" lining (Chapter X, Method One). (The panne′ velvet used in the model egg was too thin to make good cording, so I used a non-metalic braid that matched the velvet instead. You may do it either way.) Cut a small hole in the center of the velvet for the key to fit through. Use a dab of tacky to hold it in place.

10. Do the raised decoupage following the directions in Chapter XI, part 13. (See Fig. 26 for what portion of the print to use.) This project calls for only one print, but you will find it helpful to have a second one to use for reference while you are applying the first.

11. With the print raised on the egg (it doesn't have to look just like the model!), you are ready to shade with the chalks. Continue following the directions in Chapter XI. Use dark brown chalks for shadows, adding greens, yellows and even a slight amount of rose. Remember, a little goes a long way, and it can easily be over-done! Wipe off any excess with a damp cloth.

12. Using a small, round paint brush, paint a few stems or branches (optional), and sign and date the egg.

13. Carefully put a coat of Egg Sheen over the entire egg. (If you rub the egg with the brush or go over an area too much, the chalk will smear.)

14. Coat the raised portion until it is stiffened, being careful not to get Egg Sheen on the egg itself. (Note: It is alright to get Egg Sheen on the egg between close-fitting pieces of the print, but it will show and look messy if you get it anywhere else.)

15. Let the Egg Sheen dry thoroughly and put two coats of

Deep Flex Bisque Glaze over the entire egg. This will give it a matte finish and protect it.

16. Now for the final trimmings! Around the base of the handle put a row of round gold cord, followed by a row of rhinestone chain and another row of cord. Use Tacky for this.

17. Glue gold cord on the cut edge at the bottom of the egg, so the egg will sit on the cord and not on its raw edge. (This will also hide ragged places left from cutting.) On the side of the egg, at the edge, glue a row of rhinestone chain, and next to that another row of the gold cord. Put some glue at the joints of the cord to keep it from raveling or fraying.

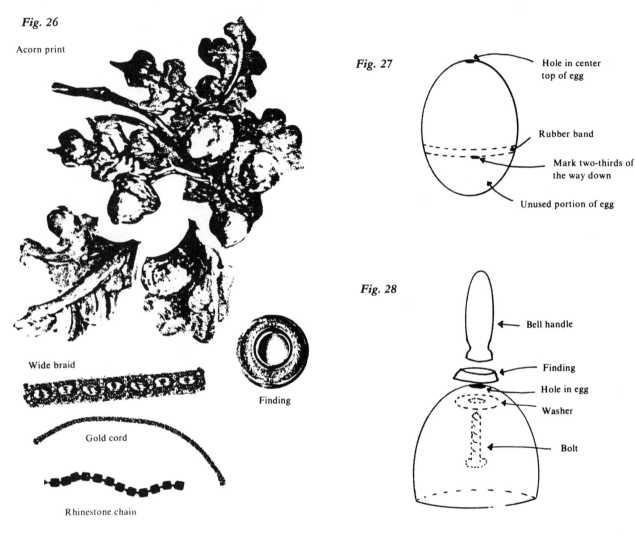

Fig. 26

Acorn print

Wide braid

Gold cord

Rhinestone chain

Finding

Fig. 27

Hole in center top of egg

Rubber band

Mark two-thirds of the way down

Unused portion of egg

Fig. 28

Bell handle

Finding

Hole in egg

Washer

Bolt

PROJECT EIGHT: BEADED JEWEL BOX

This egg is more advanced and will require the use of an electric cutting tool. An egg marker would be helpful, but is not necessary. This egg will give you experience hinging, doing the "padded" lining, and beading. The beads used on the model egg are size 12/0 "inside color" beads, meaning they are clear glass with the color in the holes. Rocailles, or any strung bead with a round shape, size 12/0 or smaller, will do. A string of beads usually measures 20" long.

1. *Supplies used:* (Fig. 29).
   Goose egg (a fat one if possible), 9 3/4" around.
   Beads: one string green, 2 strings pink, 8 strings white (Fig. 29).
   2 yards fine gold cord (Fig. 29).
   2 yards medium gold cord (Fig. 29).

Paint: white, pink, green (water-base). (Match the beads if possible).
Pink Velvet: two bias strips 1 3/4" x 18", four bias strips 5/8" x 12", and two ovals 2 x 3".
1 foot green rhinestone chain. (Match the beads).
1 hinge.
6" fine chain.
Cardboard.
Cotton ball or Fiber-Fill.
Glues: Elmer's, tacky, epoxy.
Sealer.
Stand for horizontal egg.
1/2" flat brush.

Dremel (or other electric cutting tool).
Diamond cutting disc.
Needle and thread.
3 size 20ss rhinestones. (Match rhinestone chain).

2. *Marking and cutting:*

Make a line around the egg lengthwise, a little above center. In the center front, make a dot 1/2″ below the line. Draw curving lines from the dot to the line above as shown in Fig. 30. Erase the part of the first line which is between the curving lines (Fig. 31). (The first line can be done with an egg marker, but the curving lines will have to be done freehand).

B. Position the hinge on the cutting line at the back of the egg. It should be at the fattest part of the egg with the hinge post on top of the line. Mark around it. (Follow the directions in Chapter IX for putting the hinge on one side at at time. Attach it to the top half for this project).

C. After the hinge is glued to the top half of the egg, cut the egg all the way around, using an electric cutter (See Chapter VIII).

3. Trace the pattern in Fig. 32 and transfer it to the top of your egg. Adjust the size if necessary.

4. Paint the egg, coloring the leaves green, the flowers pink, and the rest of the egg, top and bottom, white. Paint around the stems. Paint the hinge, keeping paint out of the post. Do NOT paint the area where the hinge will be glued on the bottom half of the egg.

5. Apply two coats of sealer over the paint.

6. At the very edge of the top, on the outside, glue a row of rhinestone chain, followed by a row of larger gold cord. Go over the hinge.

7. Glue size 20ss rhinestones in the centers of the flowers (Fig. 33).

8. With small gold cord, outline all the petals, leaves and stems (Fig. 33.)

9. Using Elmer's glue, glue rows of beads in the leaves and petals. There may be small gaps between some of the beads after you have put in as many as you can, but they won't show because the area below is painted the same color (Fig. 33).

10. Starting at the edge of the egg, glue rows of white beads over the rest of the top.

11. Line the inside top, following the directions in Chapter X for the "padded" lining. Put the chain in the proper position, leaving the other end free.

12. Line the bottom half next, leaving a little gap in the velvet to fit the free end of the chain into after the two halves of the egg have been joined.

13. Put the two halves of the egg together (the cording doesn't keep them from closing properly, does it??) and epoxy the hinge to the bottom half.

14. Glue a row of gold braid to the edge of the botom half, scooting it against the rhinestone chain to close any gaps. Follow this with four rows of white beads, then another row of the gold cord. Finish covering the bottom of the egg by adding rows of beads.

15. When the beads have dried, carefully epoxy the egg to the stand, trying to get it in the right position on the first try. The stand used for the model egg is the same one used for the Cradle project, only I have added pieces of a large gold finding and some rhinestones to dress it up and give the egg more stability.

16. Open the top of the egg and determine the correct length for the chain. Glue the free end in place under the velvet in the bottom half of the egg.

17. Put a little decorative item inside the lid of the jewel box, such as the lace circle with a ribbon and rhinestone in the center, as shown in the model.

Fig. 29

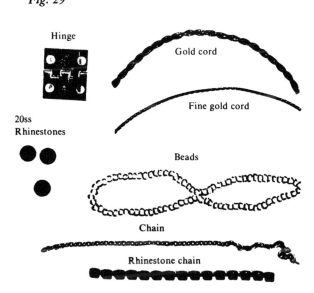

Hinge

Gold cord

Fine gold cord

20ss Rhinestones

Beads

Chain

Rhinestone chain

Fig. 30

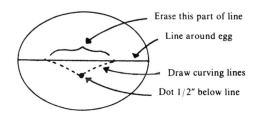

Erase this part of line

Line around egg

Draw curving lines

Dot 1/2″ below line

Fig. 31

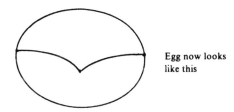

Egg now looks like this

Fig. 32

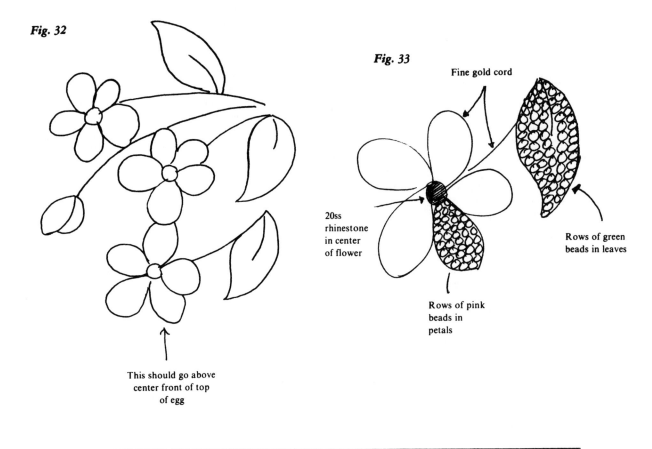

This should go above
center front of top
of egg

Fig. 33

Fine gold cord

20ss
rhinestone
in center
of flower

Rows of pink
beads in
petals

Rows of green
beads in leaves

IN CLOSING:

It is my hope, now that you have read this book, and completed all the projects (you have, haven't you?!) that you have enjoyed it and learned enough to feel comfortable with the wonderful art of egg decorating! More than that, I hope you have come to LOVE it, and that you won't stop here, but will move on to even more exciting and challenging projects.

I will be glad to help you in any way I can. Feel free to write or call, (If you are writing, be a dear and send a S.A.S.E.! Those stamps can be expensive!)

Happy Egging!

Susan Byrd

Susan Byrd
EGGS BY BYRD
HC1, Box 280
Wappapello, MO 63966
(800) 235-3447

Index

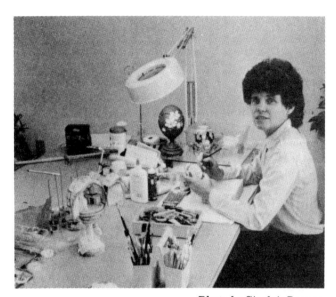

Photo by Sinclair Rogers

Susan Byrd began egg decorating as a hobby in 1966, continuing until 1978 when she began a mail-order egg supply business called "Eggs by Byrd."

If you have any questions or comments, write:

Susan Byrd
Eggs by Byrd
HC1, Box 280
Wappapello, MO 63966
(800) 235-3447